Trucking Business

How to Start, Run, and Grow an Owner
Operator Trucking Business

By: Doug Yimmer

Table of Contents

Introduction

Trucking has become a part of the culture in the United States. Most Americans have seen their share of trucking movies and television shows featuring big rigs. The trucking industry is also big business, with over 15.5 million[1] trucks registered in the United States and over 2 million drivers employed as owner-operators for big companies like Schneider, JB Hunt, Swift, and Daimler.

People are attracted to trucking for a variety of reasons. Some want to run their own business and make all the decisions; others want to be their own boss but still be able to have benefits like health insurance and paid vacation time; and some simply need a second income due to financial hardship. Whatever your reason for wanting to start an owner-operator trucking business, this book will give you the information you need to get started.

This book is designed to help you learn the basics of how to start your own trucking business. It is structured to help you get started in the trucking industry, whether you are a new driver or a new owner-operator. I will cover everything from the basics of trucking to help with your business planning and keep you on track.

---

[1] Michael (updated February 23rd 2017), available from https://usspecial.com/how-many-trucking-companies-in-the-usa/

This book will walk you through the trucking industry, from the history of trucks to the basic driver requirements. I will also give you a step-by-step guide to starting your trucking business with some great tips for new drivers and owner-operators. I will cover all the essentials for making a success of your trucking business including:

- The basics of the trucking business
- How to start a trucking company
- Finding a load or getting your own load
- How to find customers for your business as an owner-operator
- Maintenance and safety tips for new drivers
- Financing options
- Growth strategy
- And more!

So, if you're ready to get started with your own trucking business, read on and enjoy!

Chapter 1: The Trucking Industry and the Economy

The trucking industry is one of the largest industries in the U.S. Every year, trucks move an overwhelming number of products from place to place. The trucking industry is a very important part of our economy and provides jobs for hundreds of thousands of Americans.

It's also a highly competitive industry, with low profit margins and fierce competition.[2] So, you have to know what you're doing to succeed in this business, and that's exactly what this chapter will show you how to do!

The Trucking Economy, Explained

In order to succeed in the trucking industry, it's important to understand how the economy affects your business. This section will explain how your business is affected by both the national and local economies, and what you can do to protect your business from economic changes.

The National Economy

The U.S. economy as a whole is affected by things like interest rates, inflation, trade balances, and consumer confidence. These factors affect the economy by changing the demand for

---

[2] Amanda Callahan (updated April 9th, 2018), Freight trucking, general, shipping guide, available on https://www.shiplilly.com/blog/competition-heats-up-in-the-trucking-industry/

products and services, and by affecting the cost of doing business.

For example, inflation can cause[3] prices to rise when wages rise. Wage increases lead to additional spending money for consumers in addition to additional costs on businesses. These factors influence the rise in costs of goods and services. Higher prices can also be caused by higher costs of doing business, like rising transportation costs for example. In this way, the economy constantly fluctuates between periods of growth and recession (sometimes called expansions and contractions).

Interest rates are also a key indicator of the national economy. When interest rates are low, it's easier to borrow money so businesses tend to expand and hire more people. When interest rates rise, borrowing money becomes more expensive so businesses often stop expanding (or contract) in order to reduce expenses. This causes less demand for goods and services which eventually leads to recessions or even depressions (periods during which the economy shrinks or even completely collapses). That's why interest rates are a very important economic indicator for the U.S. economy as a whole!

The Local Economy

While the national economy affects all trucking companies in the U.S., local economies affect smaller areas like entire states

---

[3] Tejvan Pettinger (updated November 9th, 2019, Causes of inflation, available on https://www.economicshelp.org/macroeconomics/inflation/causes-inflation/

or even individual cities. The local economy[4] is affected by factors like the cost of fuel, availability of labor, consumer spending, and productivity.

For example, if fuel prices are high, it's more expensive to run a trucking business, so companies will have lower profits. If labor becomes more expensive, you may need to pay higher wages or hire fewer people. Either way, this will affect your ability to grow your business. If consumers aren't spending as much money on goods and services, you'll see fewer shipments and less demand for your services. Finally, if productivity falls in an area (for example if unemployment rises), then the local economy will shrink along with it!

Understanding how to use economic indicators can help you make better decisions for your business and protect yourself from economic changes that might hurt your bottom line!

The Trucking Industry

The trucking industry is made up mostly of two kinds of companies. Lease-operators and owner-operators. Lease-operators lease a truck from a company (typically an independent owner-operator) and pay them by the mile that they drive. However, there are a number of restrictions on lease-operators.

The most important restriction is that they aren't allowed to pick up and deliver loads. They can only drive for one

---

[4] Definition of local economy, available on https://www.ecnmy.org/learn/your-economics/economic-glossary/what-is-a-local-economy/

company (the lease-operator) and cannot work for any other company at the same time. This means that they don't have the flexibility or freedom to choose which loads they haul.

In addition, lease-operators don't have access to all of the best loads. The lease-operator will often get the worst loads, because they are very easy to fill up with drivers and are less attractive to load brokers. In other words, lease-operators are typically stuck with undesirable loads while owner-operators get access to better paying (and therefore more desirable) loads.

What's a Load?

A "load" is simply a shipment (a truckload) of goods that are being shipped from one place to another. For example, a load could be a box of pens being shipped from a warehouse to a store. Or it could be 500 cases of soda being shipped from one distributor to another.

The trucking industry is filled with hundreds of thousands of loads every day, and all of those loads are available to owner-operators who are looking for work. Loads can also come in different sizes. Sometimes there are small loads that only need one driver, while other times there are large loads that require multiple drivers (called "team drivers") to complete the job.

There are several different kinds of loads that you can haul, including:

Truckload

This is the largest type of load and you will have to pick up and deliver all the freight yourself. A truckload shipment consists of 1–45 trailers[5] (or more). This is typically an entire shipment being moved from one place to another by truck, therefore these shipments have higher weight limits than van or flatbed loads. For example, some truckload shipments can weigh over 80,000 pounds! If you're hauling a truckload shipment for a company (like the kind you'll be doing when you start your own business) then they will pay you by the mile that you drive.

Van

This type of load is smaller than a full truckload shipment and typically consists of a fewer number of trailers. It can be a single shipment that you haul from one place to another, or it can be a number of shipments that you pick up from several different locations and deliver to the same destination. Van loads are typically smaller than truckloads, and therefore cheaper.

Flatbed

This type of load requires you to carry a number of different types of freight on your flatbed trailer. For example, these loads could include furniture, boats, motorcycles, ATVs, or other heavy items that don't fit in a regular trailer. Because these loads require you to carry multiple types of freight on your truck, they generally have higher weight limits than

---

[5] Matt Goddyn (updated November 12th, blog on CSA transportation, available on
https://www.csatransportation.com/blog/what's-full-truckload

truckload or van loads. For example, some flatbed shipments can weigh over 40,000[6] pounds!

Hazardous Materials

This type of load (or H-Load) is similar to a truckload load except that it must be transported under special conditions (called Hazardous Material Regulations[7]). These are typically the most dangerous kinds of loads because they require the driver to follow strict safety regulations when transporting them. For example, some hazardous materials cannot be transported during certain weather conditions (such as extreme heat or cold), or they may require special permits from the government before being transported through certain cities and states.

External Factors

While factors like interest rates, inflation, and fuel prices are important, they aren't the only things that affect your business! In this section, you'll learn about other important external factors that you need to know about, including:

Legal Concerns

There are many laws[8] that affect your trucking business. You need to know what they are and how they affect the way you

---

[6] Becky Harris (updated April 12th 2017, flatbed trailers, available on https://arcb.com/blog/flatbed-trailer-shipping

[7] U.S Department of Regulations, available from https://www.phmsa.dot.gov/standards-rulemaking/hazmat/hazardous-materials-regulations

[8] Federal Trucking Laws and Regulations, available on https://www.legalinfo.com/content/truck-accidents/federal-trucking-laws-and-regulations.html

do business. Things like speed limits, traffic laws, and safety standards all have an impact on how you conduct your business.

Regulatory Agency

Every state has a state agency like the DOT (Department of Transportation) or DMV (Department of Motor Vehicles). These agencies have a lot of regulatory power over who can operate trucks and what they can do. Trucking companies need to know how these agencies work and how they can affect you.

Safety Concerns

Safety is a very important issue in the trucking industry. There are many laws that affect your ability to run a safe business and protect yourself and your clients. You need to know about each of these safety laws in order to stay out of trouble with the law.

Interest Rates

It's important to understand how changes in interest rates affect your business, especially if you have a lot of debt. In this section, you'll learn about the relationship between interest rates and small businesses. When interest rates go up, it becomes more expensive to borrow money so people will stop spending more on goods and services. This means less demand for products and services because people are spending less money on them. As a result, small businesses that depend on credit are likely to suffer higher losses than companies that don't rely on credit as much.

Fuel Prices

When fuel prices rise, it can cause problems for truckers because they're affected by fuel price fluctuations just like other businesses. For example, if fuel prices rise too high, truckers may be forced to make changes in their operations (like adding additional stops or adjusting their routes). As a result, these truckers may lose some of their clients or even go out of business altogether! Truckers that use natural gas or diesel oil instead of gasoline aren't likely to see as many problems with rising fuel costs because they use cheaper fuels. But even truckers who use alternative fuels[9] are affected by fluctuations in fuel prices because they still buy their fuel from a truck stop or gas station.

Inflation

Another important factor that affects your bottom line is inflation. In this section, you'll learn about how inflation affects your business and how you can keep your business from being hurt by rising prices. For example, inflation can cause customers to pay more for goods and services. This is especially true when it comes to products like food and fuel that people need every day. As a result, customers may stop buying as many products or they may reduce the amount of money they spend on each product. While this can be tough for businesses, rising prices also mean higher profits for truckers!

---

[9] J.E. Kim and Y.H. Percival Zhang, Alternative transportation fuels, available on
https://www.sciencedirect.com/topics/engineering/alternative-transportation-fuels.

Inflation also causes costs to rise for businesses (like trucking companies). If you're dependent on credit to finance your business, then rising costs make it harder to pay off debts. In the trucking industry, this can lead to lower profits or even bankruptcy if you have too much debt! However, if you don't rely on credit as much then rising costs won't affect you as badly—but even truckers who don't have large debts should be wary of the dangers of too much debt! For example, when inflation is high, it's better to cut costs instead of making more money. That way you can keep your profits even if inflation rises!

Labor Costs

Labor costs can also affect your business. For example, if you have union employees, you may have to pay higher wages or salaries to keep your workers happy. This can affect your business in several ways—for example, it may reduce the amount of money you earn as a result of labor costs. But even if this doesn't happen, higher labor costs can cause you to hire fewer workers or pay your workers less money.

However, it's important to realize that high labor costs may not always be bad for businesses. If productivity is low then it's better to hire a few less people and pay them more so they work harder. This will help increase productivity and make your business more profitable! Just be sure that you don't overpay your employees—otherwise they may stop working hard enough.

Another factor that affects trucking businesses is consumer spending on goods and services. When consumer spending goes up, businesses like trucking companies see an increase in demand for their services. This is especially true when there are fewer competing products like airlines or trains (for example). In this case, a company like a railroad would see an increase in demand for their products while the demand for air freight would go down. This would cause a railroad company to hire more workers, while an airline company might need to lay off employees!

On the other hand, when consumer spending goes down, businesses like trucking companies face lower demand for their products and services. This can lead to layoffs and even business closures if the downturn lasts long enough! Truckers who own their own trucks might be hit the hardest by declining consumer spending because they'll have to pay for maintenance on their trucks even if they're not making enough money!

Total Addressable Market

The total addressable market is the size of the potential market for a trucking business. For example, if the total addressable market is $100 Billion, that means there is a potential for $100 Billion in revenue (or profit) from trucking.

The total addressable market for a new trucking business will depend on the demand for its products and services. The more profitable the product and service is, the larger the total addressable market will be.

As of 2021, the total addressable market for trucking is estimated to be $700 Billion[10]. The total addressable market for trucking is expected to grow from $700 Billion in 2021 to $1 Trillion[11] by 2026.

The factors that will have the biggest impact on the size of the total addressable market are:

1. The economy (recession or expansion)
2. The cost of fuel (if fuel prices drop, more freight can be shipped)
3. Minimum wage increases (if minimum wages rise, it will increase operating costs and decrease profit margins)

In general, there will always be an economic need for freight transportation in the United States. As long as people buy stuff and need to get it from one place to another, there will always be a need for freight transportation services.

This is due to two reasons:

1. Transporting goods by trucking is much more efficient than transporting them by other means (e.g., by ship).

---

[10] Steven John (updated June 3rd 2019, Markets Insider, available on https://markets.businessinsider.com/news/stocks/trucking-industry-facts-us-truckers-2019-5-1028248577
[11] Research and markets (updated November 6th 2020), available on https://www.globenewswire.com/news-release/2020/11/06/2121823/0/en/Global-Freight-Trucking-Market-2020-2027-U-S-Market-is-Estimated-at-1-1-Trillion-While-China-is-Forecast-to-Grow-at-7-2-CAGR.html

2. Trucks are much more versatile than any other means of transportation. Compared to other means of transport such as ships, trucking provides more flexible options regarding transports routes and time schedules and is relatively cheaper compared to ocean freights.

Because freight transportation is one of the most efficient and most cost-effective forms of transportation, there will always be a need for it in the economy as long as people buy stuff and need to get it from one place to another. As long as people buy things, there will always be a need for freight transportation services in the United States (and in every country).

The size of the total addressable market depends on two factors:

Economic Growth

It doesn't matter how good your product or service is if people don't have an economic need for it. If people don't have an economic need for your product or service, you will not be able to make any money through your business because you won't have any customers (or a market).

As a business owner, you should focus on serving the needs of people and addressing economic needs. You will then be able to serve your customers' needs profitably. This will help you make money in the long run.

For example, if people don't have an economic need for your product or service, you won't be able to sell it and make money through your business. In that case, it doesn't matter how good your product or service is; it simply won't get sold and you won't be able to make any money from it. This will result in a loss for your business (and you).

If people have an economic need for your product or service, they will buy it because they see value in it (they recognize its benefits). When people buy things that they see value in (that solve their problems), they feel good about themselves. This is because they are getting value for their hard-earned dollars. This feeling of self-worth makes them happy and creates a positive feeling inside them (which makes them want to continue doing business with you). In other words, if people have an economic need for your product or service, they will feel good about doing business with you.

Fuel Prices

Fuel prices have a big impact on the total addressable market for trucking. The reason for this is because fuel is a big expense for trucking companies. As fuel prices increase, freight transportation becomes less profitable and the total addressable market shrinks.

During times of high fuel price, freight transportation companies are squeezed at both ends:

1. They have to pay more for fuel (which means they have to charge more for their services to make a profit). This results in them not being able to undercut their competitors by charging lower rates than them. In this scenario, they lose a lot of business because they can't compete on price with other trucking companies

that charge lower rates due to having lower operating costs (other than fuel expenses).

2. They also lose business because customers choose other forms of transportation since it is cheaper than freight transportation (since it has lower operating costs). For example, if customers hire planes or LTL companies instead of using trucks, trucks will make less money and be forced to charge higher rates in order to make a profit. This will cause them to lose even more business (and cause the total addressable market to shrink even more).

When fuel prices increase, the total addressable market shrinks because companies struggle to make a profit. This is due to the fact that fuel prices increase operating expenses for trucking companies and shrink the profit margins (which means they can't undercut their competitors by charging lower rates than them). An increase in fuel prices will inevitably lead to an increase in freight transportation rates, which will inhibit the ability to attract new businesses and new customers.

Employee Turnover Rates

The turnover rate for the trucking industry is higher than most industries. More trucks are sold in the U.S. than any other industry, but new drivers are needed to operate those trucks. The turnover rate in the trucking industry is approximately 98%[12] per year, which is especially high.

Two reasons for this high turnover rate are:

---

[12] Roger Gilroy (updated October 11th 2018) available from https://www.ttnews.com/categories/driver-turnover.

1. Due to the trucking industry having a negative reputation, many of the new drivers who enter the industry decide to leave after a short time because they don't like it.
2. The pay is not as high in the trucking industry as it is in other industries, such as construction and manufacturing; therefore, many drivers who are used to making $8-$15[13] an hour decide that they would rather make over $16[14] an hour working in construction or manufacturing.

Due to this high turnover rate, most trucking companies have experienced drivers who have been around for a while and have become accustomed to the lifestyle of trucking. Most companies hire new drivers by advertising through job fairs and training schools. If you are looking for a career with continuous opportunity, then becoming a professional driver would be perfect for you. Truck driving will give you freedom that most jobs won't give you. You will be your own boss, work when you want, and go where you want. And if you don't like it after a while, then simply quit and find another job somewhere else (which is relatively easy).

As such, the turnover rate in the trucking industry is high due to the fact that most drivers who enter the industry, don't like it, and thus leave. The turnover rate can also be high due to

---

[13] Truck Driving salary per hour, available on https://www.alltrucking.com/faq/per-hour-salary.
[14] Average PayScale, available on https://www.payscale.com/research/US/Job=Construction_Work er/Hourly_Rate

the type of people who are attracted to the industry. Some of these people have been fired from other jobs and/or have other reasons for leaving their last job.

Risks and Other Considerations

Trucking is not something that someone should enter into blindly. There are significant risks involved and one should understand all of them. This includes the risk of an accident that might result in personal injury or death, uninsured/underinsured motorists, theft, vandalism, and office related problems such as excessive phone calls, a computer malfunctioning, or even a fax machine breaking down.

Be aware of all of the risks and potential problems before you enter into this business.

Another factor to consider is your competition. Trucking is a big industry with many large companies that offer the same type of services as you are providing through your trucking business. Many large companies have established advertising campaigns on television and radio, along with billboards and other marketing plans to attract new customers to their company. This can make it difficult for a new owner-operator trucking company to compete against the larger companies because they often have more money available than a small independent trucker does in order to promote their business.

However, this does not mean that small owner-operator trucking businesses cannot be successful in competing against big companies. These smaller businesses can be as successful as the larger companies if they concentrate on their strengths and develop their business methods around those strengths, rather than trying to match the larger companies' business plans.

Be aware of your competition and try to understand how they are marketing their company. Use this information to determine how you should market your company as well.

Here are the major risk considerations that are involved in trucking:

Insurance Risks

Most truckers are required to carry a minimum level of liability insurance for their truck. This is usually a million dollars per occurrence. This insurance protects the driver and also protects their customers in the event that there is an accident. There are other types of insurance that may be required depending upon the type of cargo being hauled. If you are hauling any type of hazardous material, you will need to carry additional insurance to protect yourself and others from any potential danger that might occur due to the transporting of these materials.

Most drivers carry additional insurance beyond what is required by law because they want to protect themselves from as many situations as possible. If they can avoid putting themselves at risk by carrying an extra policy, they try to do so because it is less expensive than paying out in case something does happen and they become responsible for it.

As an owner-operator, you will need to decide whether or not your company will require its drivers to purchase additional insurance policies beyond what is state-required. This will depend upon how much risk you think your drivers are taking on with the loads they haul and how much money those loads may be worth if there were some type of accident.

Personal Injury vs. Property Damage

The majority of trucking accidents occur when the truck hits something. This can be another vehicle, a pedestrian, a building, or other stationary object. The majority of these accidents result in property damage only, but there are also many that result in personal injury or even death. If someone is killed or injured as a result of an accident involving your company's truck, you will be held responsible for the damages that are incurred because your driver was operating your truck at the time of the accident.

This liability insurance will protect you from being sued for any damages that might occur from these types of accidents. If your driver causes an accident and it is found that he was intoxicated or under the influence of drugs, you will also need to be carrying additional insurance to protect yourself from these types of situations. You may need to modify how you conduct business in order to protect yourself and your drivers from illegal substances and alcohol use by them while they are on company time behind the wheel. This will include having a drug testing policy in place that requires your drivers to take drug tests before they begin work, as well as anytime they have made an error on their logs or if they have been involved in an accident while operating your truck.

Theft

Many drivers, especially those that are new to the industry, do not realize how easy it is for someone to steal their truck while it is parked at a rest stop or while they are eating at a restaurant. This type of theft is called an "inside job" because the person that steals the vehicle knows the security codes and can often gain access to the vehicles in a matter of minutes without being noticed by anyone else around. They will then drive your company's truck well away from where they stole it in order to make sure it cannot be found easily. This is also known as joyriding and is much more common than most people think that it is. It can also be very expensive if you find yourself having to replace your vehicle because someone stole it from you.

One way that you can prevent this type of theft is by installing a GPS tracking device on your truck. These devices are small enough to be hidden somewhere inside of your truck and will alert you if something happens with your vehicle—even if someone has stolen it from you and has been able to change its VIN number or license plate before the crime has been reported to law enforcement officials.

Vandalism and other problems with vandalism can also occur if your truck is parked for a period of time on the street. If you do not have a company lot or some other secure location where your truck can be parked, you will need to take extra precautions to protect it from damage and theft. You will want to remove any company logos from the exterior of your truck as well as the interior. This will prevent someone from breaking into it and stealing any of your equipment or supplies that may be inside. They may also steal items they find inside your truck such as purses, wallets, cell phones, computers, and other items that are easily taken when they are left unattended in a vehicle.

One other thing you can do to protect against theft and vandalism is to install a security system in the cab of your truck that will protect all of your equipment that is kept there. This can help prevent anyone from breaking into the cab of your truck while you are away from it.

Finally, as an owner-operator business owner, you should make sure that all doors on your truck lock properly so that no one can force them open while you are away from the vehicle. You should also make sure that no one can break out any windows in order to gain access inside of your truck.

Crime is a major problem in many parts of the country and you need to be aware of the potential problems that can occur in your area. If you are operating your business in an area where there are high crime rates, you will need to take extra precautions to protect yourself and your truck from theft or vandalism.

The Future of Trucking

The trucking industry is the backbone of the economy. It is responsible for moving more than 70% of domestic freight and goods across the country. It provides jobs and a livelihood for over 3.5 million[15] people, most who are part-time drivers.

---

[15] Jennifer Cheeseman day and Andrew W. Hait (updated June 6th 2019), available on https://www.census.gov/library/stories/2019/06/america-keeps-on-trucking.html

The industry as a whole generates $700 billion[16] in sales annually.

Unfortunately, it is also one of the most dangerous industries in America, especially for truck drivers. Over 4,000[17] people die every year in truck related accidents. Many more are injured or permanently disabled in these accidents.

The demand for trucking has grown rapidly since the early 2000s, especially from e-commerce concerns such as Amazon and Walmart that want to deliver their products faster and cheaper to the consumer using giant shipping containers on trucks owned by carriers like FedEx, UPS, JB Hunt, and others. This has created a fierce competition between these companies that has only gotten worse over time due to the high cost of fuel and other expenses, like equipment depreciation and insurance premiums, that have caused carriers to make less money on every mile they drive across country—which explains why many carriers are now looking at alternative means to deliver their goods such as using airplanes or even unmanned drones, as this will save them time and money.

However, as mentioned earlier, one of the biggest challenges facing the trucking industry is finding new drivers. This is largely due to the fact that the job of a truck driver has evolved into a more dangerous one and this has caused many people

---

[16] Sean McNally (updated August 19th), available from https://www.trucking.org/news-insights/new-report-finds-trucking-industry-revenues-topped-700-billion

[17] Kevin Jones (updates December 21st 2016), available from https://www.trucker.com/drivers/media-gallery/21745964/truck-drivers-top-latest-work-fatality-list

to shy away from it. In fact, drivers in the trucking industry have an extremely high rate of suicide compared to other professions.

A recent study by the Center for Disease Control and Prevention found that truck drivers have a suicide rate[18] that is as high as police officers and much higher than all other professions when taking into consideration workers over all. The study was taken from a report on 2010[19] using information from the National Occupational Mortality Surveillance database from the National Institute for Occupational Safety and Health.

Startups like Embark are attempting to solve this problem by automating truck driving with self-driving trucks. This has the potential to put many truck drivers out of work, but it will also help companies like Amazon and Walmart get their goods to consumers faster and cheaper.

These startups are not alone. Large carriers such as JB Hunt and UPS are also looking to replace drivers with autonomous trucks.[20] In fact, UPS has already tested the technology in a number of their trucks throughout the country.

---

[18] Jessica Ferger (Updated March 17th 2015), available from https://www.cbsnews.com/media/suicide-in-the-workplace-which-professions-are-high-risk/
[19] NOMS, available from https://www.cbsnews.com/media/suicide-in-the-workplace-which-professions-are-high-risk/
[20] Katie Burke (updated February 4th 2021), available from https://blogs.nvidia.com/blog/2021/02/04/what-is-autonomous-truck/

Another reason for this is that a shortage of drivers is forcing many companies to invest in more efficient shipping methods such as low-cost, smaller trucking companies that use fewer truck drivers; more automated trucks will help them overcome this problem and reduce their operating costs. This is also raising concerns among drivers who fear that they will be replaced by robots driving trucks around the country at all hours of the day.

However, it will take some time for self-driving trucks to replace all of the drivers in America, especially due to the complicated nature of state laws regarding self-driving cars. Still, it is not unrealistic to believe that automated vehicles could eventually put over 4.4 million[21] Americans out of work which would drastically affect our economy.

This is why it is extremely important for trucking companies and other businesses in the industry to find new ways to attract new drivers as well as find ways to keep them safe on the road so they can continue making deliveries on time and get paid for their hard work.

Having said that, there is still a large upside and potential to be in the trucking industry now given that the increase in freights and consumerism is booming in an age of online shopping.

Now, let's take a look at how you can take the first step in starting your own trucking business.

---

[21] Sean Kilcarr (updated May 31st 2017), available from https://www.fleetowner.com/technology/article/21696130/report-driverless-trucks-will-eliminate-millions-of-jobs

Chapter 2: Getting Started

This chapter discusses how to start your own trucking business. This is where a lot of people get stuck. They want to start their own business and yet they make it very difficult for themselves.

The first thing you need to do is to understand your role as an owner-operator.

The Role of the Owner-Operator

One of the most important roles you will play in your business is that of owner-operator, and it is crucial that you understand the importance of this role to your future success. As an owner-operator, you are responsible for all the operations of your business. You will be responsible for all the decisions that affect your business, ranging from how much to charge for your services to how to spend the money you earn. If you are not willing or able to accept this responsibility, then you should not operate as an independent owner-operator.

The role of owner-operator is also important because it gives you a degree of freedom not usually found in most other businesses. While some businesses limit their owner's freedom in various ways, and others force their owners into a limited number of roles, the independent owner-operator business puts its owner into a unique position: one where he or she has total control over the outcome of his or her business. This is why so many people decide to start trucking businesses; they want to have complete control over their own destinies.

As an independent owner-operator, you have total freedom over how much money you make and even if you make money at all! No one will force you into any particular role if you don't want it—but if there is someone who would be willing to do so, then it probably isn't worth doing! If someone tells you that you need to do something a certain way because "that's how it always has been done" or "that's the way it works," then that should raise a big red flag. In the world of business, there is no such thing as the one right way of doing things. Whatever works best for you is what you should do!

This freedom can carry some risks, though, and so it is important to be aware of them. As an independent owner-operator, you are responsible for your own success or failure. It is up to you to make sure your business succeeds, and if it fails, then the blame will not be placed on anyone else. This means that you need to control every element of your business in order to make sure that everything runs smoothly; if there are any problems, then they will be yours and yours alone.

The freedom associated with being an independent owner-operator also comes with responsibilities that many people may not be aware of. In addition to all the other responsibilities involved in running a business (such as transportation planning or revenue forecasting), an owner-operator must take care of all his or her own legal and financial matters when starting a new trucking business. This includes things like figuring out how to incorporate or form a limited liability company, deciding how to set up your finances, and figuring out how you will pay your taxes. You must also take care of things like insurance and compliance with various regulations.

Finally, it is important to remember that you must be patient; the trucking business is not a get-rich-quick scheme. If you are willing to do the work necessary to start a successful business, and if you are willing to be persistent in the face of failure, then you will find success in this industry—but only if you are willing and able to commit yourself 100% to the long-term success of your business.

Initial Startup Capital

The amount of money you need to start a business will depend on the type of business you are starting and the size of your business. Some trucking businesses are very small and only require a single truck and some equipment, while others require a larger initial investment in equipment and assets.

All businesses need capital to start, but not all capital is created equal. Certain types of capital are much more important than others when it comes to starting a trucking business. For example, it is possible to get started in the business with zero cash on hand (or perhaps just a few thousand dollars), but if you do not have any working capital, then your chances of succeeding as an owner-operator will be very slim. By working capital, I mean the cash that is necessary to cover expenses like fuel and insurance during your first few months in business— when you don't have enough money coming in to cover all your costs. Without any working capital in these early months, you will have no choice but to load up your truck with whatever freight is available at low rates—which may or may not pay for all your operating costs.

For most new owner-operators, the majority of their initial investment must go toward working capital so that they can start their business with the cash that is necessary to keep their business running. As a rule of thumb, most new owner-operators should have between $50,000 and $60,000 in working capital when they start their business. This is enough to cover expenses for a few months and also provide a buffer so that you do not run out of money if there happens to be an unexpected expense or delay in getting paid. This money can come from any number of sources, but the most common place for most owner-operators to get it is from their own savings or retirement funds.

While it's fine and dandy to have enough working capital when you start your business, we all know that $50,000 or more isn't going to last forever—especially if you don't make any money! That's why it is important to quickly turn your capital into revenue so that you can keep your business running. The best way I've found for doing this is by leveraging the power of the trucking brokerage industry in my favor.

In order to understand how this works, we must first take a look into how transportation brokers work and how they help independent owner-operators find freight.

Freight Brokers

Most people are familiar with the term "broker" when it comes to trucking. Most people assume that trucking brokers are just middlemen who take a fee for arranging deals between shippers and carriers. While this is true, they also serve an important role in the trucking industry that goes beyond simply connecting shippers with carriers.

When a shipper needs freight moved from point A to point B, a broker will search his or her database to find a carrier willing to haul the load who is going in the right direction, has the right equipment, and has capacity on their trucks. The broker then presents all of this information to the shipper and charges a fee for his or her services. This is all well and good, but there is a way brokers can be used by owner-operators instead of vice versa!

Instead of using brokers as customer service agents, you can use them as your own agents! If you have not yet made any money in your business, then it may not be possible for you to attract customers on your own—especially if you don't have much experience in the industry. This is where brokerage firms can help; by working with a good brokerage firm, you can essentially buy your own customer relationships. A good brokerage firm will have a large database of shippers that they already have a good working relationship with. These shippers are usually willing to work with brokers because it gives them access to more capacity than they would normally have on their own; by using brokers, they don't have to waste time haggling with individual owner-operators about prices and loads—the broker handles all that!

When you work with a brokerage firm, one of the first things you will do is make a deal with them about how much capacity they will allocate to you each month. For example, if you make an agreement that they will provide you with 20,000 miles of capacity per month, then it is up to you to find the freight to fill it! This can be hard for new owner-operators who do not have much experience in the industry or many contacts; many brokerages expect new owner-operators to bring their own customers as well as their own freight!

If this sounds like something that might be difficult for you, then I recommend that you use the services of a brokerage firm like us at MajorFreight.com! They are a brokerage firm that specializes in helping owner-operators find freight and start their businesses. They have a large network of shippers who have specifically requested to work with owner-operators like you, and they give you access to all of this capacity without asking you for any money up front. All you need to do is provide them with enough information about your trucking business and they will handle the rest!

There is a catch, however; brokerage firms like MajorFreight.com will work with you and your business in exchange for a percentage of your revenue. This means that you will only get paid if there are shippers willing to pay to have freight transported by you—which is why it is so important to have a good broker working with you! If they can't find shippers willing to pay for your service, then you won't make any money off of your business—and that means that neither will they!

Other than brokers, you can also get your initial capital from a bank loan, but this is not recommended. The problem with bank loans is that they usually have very high interest rates and are not easy to qualify for. You won't have any problems qualifying for a trucking loan if you have a good credit score and some cash in your business, but the interest rates will probably be too high to make it worthwhile. If you want to get a loan, then you should use your money to get more equipment or assets so that your business becomes more profitable—not pay high interest on a loan from the bank!

Here are some of the main expenses involved in starting any type of a business:

Business License and Taxes

Most cities and states require that you pay a business license fee and taxes on your home address as well. You have to pay local, state, and federal taxes on your home address. This is just part of owning a business. Many newbie trucking business owners do not realize this when they get started with their new business venture.

If you are going to operate out of your home, you will have to apply for a business license with your city or county clerk's office in the area where you live, as well as paying sales tax on any supplies that you purchase for your business from either your residence or where you plan to operate out of. You will have to apply for an occupational tax license with the state that you will be operating out of before doing so as well.

Office Space Rental

If you plan to rent office space for your new trucking company, that will be one more expense that is associated with getting started with an owner-operator trucking company. If you don't want to rent office space, then I would suggest getting started out of your home office or garage.

If you decide to start out of your home, you can always convert a part of your home into a business office. This way you will not have to pay any rent, and you will not have to worry about going to work in the rain or snow, so it's a win-win situation for everyone.

Truck Purchase

The next expense that would be involved with starting a trucking business is the purchase of the truck needed to run your business. If you are an experienced owner-operator driver who already owns their own truck, this expense will be much lower for you than if you decided to purchase one from scratch. If this is the case, then I suggest buying one that is already set up as a cab and chassis, which may cost more initially but it will save you money on insurance costs as well as getting set up on the road faster since all it needs is a motor put in it. You can also purchase one from an auction house where many trucks are sold off cheap because they were written off due to being involved in an accident and they need repairs before they can be sold again, or they are just too old and need repairs that are not cost effective for the owner to invest in them anymore.

If you are starting a new trucking business from scratch, then you should consider purchasing a used truck that is already set up with a cab and chassis. If you find a truck that has been built within the last five years or so, then you will not have to worry about it having many of the mechanical problems that older trucks have. This way, you will be able to get your business started sooner since the only thing that it will need done is putting in your motor and other parts for the truck.

Motor Purchase

If you already own your own truck, then this expense can be skipped, but if you do not own one or are buying one, then this expense can be quite high if you buy one new off of a dealership lot. If you want to start your business as cheaply as possible, then I would suggest finding one at an auction house or from another owner-operator driver who is selling his motor for an older model truck or cab and chassis combo. This way, once again, it will save money on insurance costs too, since they are usually undervalued when sold at auction like this.

Truck Insurance

Trucking insurance can be quite expensive at times, which is another reason why I suggest buying a truck that has already been set up with a cab and chassis. If you do not own your own truck, then you will need to buy this insurance as well as cover the cost of your truck. Many independent owner-operator drivers do not have their own insurance on their trucks and instead pay for a blanket policy for the company that they are driving for at the time. This way they can drive for any company that they want to, without having to worry about finding insurance or being turned down by an insurance company since they are considered high risk.

If you want to try and keep your costs down as much as possible when starting out, then I would suggest doing this as well. You can always purchase your own truck later on once you know that the business is going to succeed in order to save money on high insurance rates once again.

Maintenance costs can be quite high depending on how often you plan on having your truck worked on or serviced by someone else. If you plan on doing service maintenance yourself, there are many books available where you can learn how to do it yourself cheap and easy. Some books also cover basics like how to change your oil and air filter, which can save you some money on maintenance costs.

If you choose to have someone else do the regular maintenance, then you will have to pay them for the time and labor that they put into it as well as paying for the parts that they use. This can add up to quite a bit of money over time. If you choose this option, then I would suggest finding a mechanic that has worked on semi-trucks before because it usually will cost less if they have worked on one since they know what part of the engine or truck is causing the problem.

Vehicle Selection and Acquisition

The first thing an-owner operator needs to do is select the right vehicle for his business. As with any other business, it's crucial to have the right tools for the job. Here are a few suggestions:

Buy a truck that will hold its value. The industry standard is to buy a truck that can survive at least 500,000 miles. Buy something that's built well and capable of surviving on the road for years. The last thing you want is to be stuck with a beat-up truck, so buy one that's in great shape!

Get something with some power behind it. A good idea is getting something with a diesel engine. This will give you better gas mileage and more power than similar trucks with gasoline engines. A diesel engine will also last much longer than a gasoline engine; which means it'll be able to withstand rougher roads and conditions while still maintaining good fuel economy (a diesel engine uses about 30% more fuel than its gasoline counterpart, but gains back this difference on longevity). Diesel engines also don't require as much maintenance as gasoline engines; yet they're capable of greater torque and horsepower output, making them ideal for hauling heavy loads on uneven terrain (typically in hilly areas). A diesel engine will also run just fine in freezing temperatures, which can be a problem for gasoline engines (a good rule of thumb is to keep your fuel tank at least half full or else you run the risk of your engine not starting due to the fuel gelling).

Get a truck with an automatic transmission. You'll save yourself a lot of time and effort by having an automatic transmission. Although it's more expensive, it'll be worth it in the long-run since it gives you more time to make money and less time spent on mechanical work (so you can focus on running your business). This also helps you get better gas mileage, which is especially helpful if you have to travel long distances between destinations.

Get one with a sleep section and a shower. As an owner-operator, you will come across many opportunities where you can earn extra income by driving other people around. By having a place for passengers/clients to sleep and shower, they'll be much more likely to travel with you again since they had an enjoyable experience on their trip. Plus, this helps bring in more revenue for your business!

In addition to getting something with a diesel engine and automatic transmission, get one that's roomy and has lots of storage space. This will come in handy when you need to carry supplies for your business.

Before you buy the vehicle, be sure to evaluate it carefully and make sure everything is in good working condition. You don't want to go through the hassle of selling a truck later on only to find out that it was too expensive to maintain or had some major problem that you failed to notice. If there's something wrong with the truck, make sure it's fixed before you purchase it!

Also, make sure you get a good amount of coverage from your insurance company. As an owner-operator, your truck will be your home away from home—so make sure your insurance covers everything (including: tires, engine parts, electrical parts, etc.). You might also want to look into an umbrella policy (which provides liability coverage) and disability insurance (which protects you against chronic health problems). Don't forget about additional protection for things like: flood damage, fire damage, theft, vandalism, etc. You should also keep in mind that if someone gets hurt while on your property or while riding in your vehicle, their medical bills and related expenses could cost you thousands of dollars; so, it's important that you're covered for these types of situations as well.

Business Registration

There are two types of business registration. They are sole proprietorship or LLC. We recommend you to register your business as an LLC.

What is a sole proprietorship?

Sole proprietorship is when the company is owned by one individual. The sole proprietor is personally liable for all the debts and obligations of the business. One can register a sole proprietorship as an LLC; however, it is not mandatory.

What is an LLC?

Limited liability company (LLC) is a legal structure that combines the pass-through taxation of a partnership or sole proprietorship with the limited liability of a corporation. It offers limited liability to its owners in that they are not personally liable for any claim or debt made against the LLC and are thus insulated from potential lawsuits against the business. In fact, only the assets of an LLC can be seized, not personal assets, unless those are directly connected to company operations such as loans from personal bank accounts. An LLC may elect to have tax treatment as either a "pass-through" entity or as a corporation, depending on any number of factors including tax considerations and owner-members' preferences. A pass-through entity does not pay corporate taxes separately from its owners; instead, it "passes through" income or losses to its owners, who then report their share of income or loss on their personal tax returns. Taxes for LLCs are determined by the state in which it is created, and also by the number of members possessing an interest in the LLC.

Sole Proprietorship vs. LLC

The sole proprietorship is the best choice for a one-person business, whereas an LLC is appropriate for a business with two or more owners. An LLC may offer tax benefits as well as limited liability. It's not that hard to start an LLC. You can form one by filing articles of organization with your state's incorporation office and paying an annual registration fee. As long as you don't employ any employees, you can operate an LLC totally under the radar without ever registering with your state's secretary of state or hiring a lawyer to draft your operating agreement or buying a company seal for your stationary.

The process to start an LLC is very simple. You can follow these steps:

Draft a Legal Document, Known as the Operating Agreement

This specifies the rules for your LLC's operation and the allocation of its assets and liabilities in case of a future dissolution. The operating agreement should be approved by all members of the LLC before or shortly after it is formed (most states do not require that you file the operating agreement with your state government). Some states may require you to file a copy of your LLC's operating agreement with the state, but this is usually not required in most states.

Apply for an EIN from IRS-Online Form SS-4 (Application for Employer Identification Number)

If your LLC has employees or will have employees at any time in its existence, you will need to have an EIN (Employer Identification Number). You can apply for one online through

IRS-Online Form SS-4 (Application for Employer Identification Number). It takes about five minutes to fill out the form online and it is free. If you want to file your taxes online, you will need to have an EIN.

File for Your LLC Name Trademark

In some states (like California), you must register your LLC's name as a "fictitious business name" with the state.

Obtain a DBA License

If your business will operate under a name other than the one on your LLC's articles of organization, you should apply for an assumed business name (DBA) license to use the name. The DBA application is usually available from your city or county government.

Apply for Miscellaneous Permits

If your LLC will operate as an automobile repair shop, a home contractor, or a similar business, you will likely need to obtain a business license from your county or city government. These licenses are usually available from local government offices. Make sure you know the zoning regulations for your area before applying.

Obtain Insurance

If you will have employees or if you operate in a dangerous industry (such as construction), you should consider purchasing workers' compensation and liability insurance. You can usually obtain insurance through either an insurance agent or by contacting an insurance company directly.

Most banks and credit unions allow sole proprietors to open checking accounts with low minimum balances and no monthly fees. Be careful, though! Many banks charge high fees if they find out that the account is being used for business purposes (so don't tell them!). Some even close the accounts of sole proprietors who deposit too much money in them! So be careful when depositing money into your new business bank account (see below). Some states also impose restrictions on how much of the money in an LLC's bank account can be withdrawn by its members on a regular basis.

Four Operating Models

There are four basic business operating models that a trucking business can take.

Leasing

The first model is leasing. Leasing your truck and full-service driving for a carrier is definitely the easiest way to start a trucking business. The reason why it is the easiest to start is because you are not responsible for the maintenance and repair of your truck. You are not responsible for purchasing fuel or making sure that the truck is stocked with food products. The carrier provides everything the driver needs to get the job done. In many cases, drivers who lease their truck will work with one or two carriers, but they will have a different truck for each carrier. This allows them to take advantage of better freight rates that each carrier offers, but they also have a dedicated truck that will only run for one company.

The downside to leasing is that you will not own the truck at the end of your lease period. If you want to continue to drive for that carrier, you will have to lease another truck from them. On the other hand, if you decide that you no longer want to work for a carrier or if they no longer have a truck available for lease, then you will have to look elsewhere for a carrier.

Owner-Operator

This is the second business operating model and it is always my favorite. This means that you own your own truck and when you are not using it yourself, you can lease it out as an owner-operator. When people start out in this business model, their primary goal is typically to start out with one truck and build up their fleet size over time. This way they can earn money while they are building up their fleet size so that they can take advantage of better freight rates across the board for all of their trucks.

This business model definitely has some advantages over leasing or becoming a company driver because as an owner-operator, when your lease expires with one carrier or when the company decides they do not need your services anymore, then you can move on to another carrier and still keep driving your truck. Another benefit is that you are not responsible for the maintenance and repair of the truck. You can hire a professional or you can do the work yourself. I have personally been doing all of my own repairs and maintenance for most of my career, but I would recommend hiring a professional if you are not familiar with how to do the work. This is because there is a lot to learn when it comes to being a small business owner and being responsible for the maintenance of your truck.

Leasing Company Truck

The third model is leasing company trucks. This means that you lease your truck from the company rather than an outside carrier. In this case, the company will typically provide all of the required items needed for running your business including fuel, maintenance, repair, and food products (if food products are included in lease). The downside to this business model is that in most cases, you will only drive for their company and you will not be able to go anywhere else. In other words, if they decide they no longer want your services or if they have no more trucks available for lease, you will be out of work unless you go out on your own or find another carrier who has extra trucks available for lease. If this happens then it means that you will have to obtain your own truck and start your business from scratch.

Company Driver

This is the fourth business operating model and it is always my last choice. This means that you are an employee of a carrier who provides the truck, fuel, maintenance, repair, food products, etc. The only thing they do not provide is the driver. This is because the carrier has to abide by certain laws when it comes to hiring drivers. The only requirement for being a driver for a company is that you are over 21 years old and you have a valid CDL license with passenger and air brake endorsements. If you do not have any of those things or if you do not meet their requirements, there is no way for them to hire you as an employee. Therefore, companies will usually hire independent contractors who already meet their requirements and can take on their loads when they need them to be taken on. This means that if you are an independent contractor, it will be up to you to get yourself employed by a carrier so that they can offer their freight rates to you in order for you to earn money in this business model.

As I said before, this was always my last choice because I never wanted any type of boss or company telling me what to do. I know that there are lots of drivers who will argue with me and tell me that working for a company is better than owning your own truck because companies usually provide more benefits including medical, dental, and vision insurance. However, they also have rules and regulations that you must abide by or you will lose your job.

Now, if you are like me, you would rather be an independent contractor where you can drive for multiple companies or even be an owner-operator where you can drive your truck for multiple companies and still run your own business at the same time. That is why I have always been an independent contractor over the years because it allows me to take on as much or as little work as I want while allowing me to keep my freedom of choice when it comes to my personal life outside of driving a truck. However, if you are just starting out in this business model then it might be hard for you to find work as an independent contractor especially if no one knows who you are yet.

A big advantage to working for a company is that the company will provide you with a truck that you can lease out as an owner-operator. This means that they will provide you with everything you need to make money except for one thing, the driver. You are responsible for finding drivers and hiring them. The only thing they will do is pay your payroll taxes and give you a check each week or every other week. It is your responsibility to pay them back in the form of lease payments for their truck so that you can continue to make money from their freight rates. So if this business model sounds good to you then I highly recommend using it as long as you can find work as an independent contractor over the years; eventually, they may decide to hire you as an employee which will allow them to take care of all of your expenses including your payroll taxes and insurance costs without having to deal with leasing or owning another truck.

Why Trucking Businesses Fail

There are many reasons why trucking businesses fail. I will list some of the main reasons for you to be aware of given your experience level and where you are in your business and your financial situation.

Financing

This is one of the main reasons most trucking businesses fail. Most newbie trucking business owners do not know how to properly finance their new venture. They either have no financing, or they go out and buy a new truck or lease a truck and some equipment, and then they run out of money because they did not plan the startup financially correctly.

Most times that I speak with new owner-operators, this is one of the main problems why they are failing. They have no financial backing from the beginning of their business startup.

Not knowing how to finance your business is like walking through life without your shoes on. You will get hurt every time you take a step. The same goes for financing your business if you don't know what you are doing, or if you don't have anyone in your corner who does know what they are doing in regards to financial management for your new business venture.

If you do not have any money saved up when starting your business, or if you do not have anyone who can help you with financing your business startup, then I would suggest that you hold off on starting any type of a full-time owner-operator trucking company until you get the finances in order and ready to go before taking the final plunge.

Trying to pay off the cost of a new truck or new equipment out of your profit per mile is not a smart way to start a business. It will take several years before you make enough money to pay for all that pricey equipment you just bought.

As I stated earlier, there are other ways to purchase and finance your business startup, if you do not have the finances to do so. I will go into detail in the following chapters.

Trucking Business Startup Expenses

So what are the expenses that are involved in starting a trucking business? Well, after talking with thousands of new and veteran trucking business owners over the years through my website and through my seminars, I have discovered that most businesses fail because they are not prepared financially to start their business. Most newbie owner-operators don't know what it takes financially to start up their business and then keep it running smoothly over the long haul.

It's like going out and buying a brand-new car on credit without having any idea how much it will cost you per month for insuring and maintaining your brand new car every year for five years until it comes time for getting your next lease or buyout on your new car. You can't just go out and buy a car and expect to pay for it out of your profits without some type of a plan in place.

The same goes for starting any type of a business. It takes planning and finances to start a trucking business, and you need to be prepared financially for what is involved in starting the business.

Let's look at some typical costs involved in starting any type of a business, no matter what it may be. Say you are getting started with your new owner-operator trucking business on a part-time basis and want to keep your full-time job as well. Or maybe you have been thinking about getting started with an owner-operator company, but never really took the time to sit down and think about all that is involved in getting started before jumping into it head first.

If you are like most people, when they get ready to start their own trucking company, they lose sight of everything that is involved in running any type of a business from home, or from anywhere else for that matter, that does not have their address on the building. Most people forget about all the expenses associated with running any type of an operating business.

Chapter 3: Business Basics

As it is with most small businesses, the first step in becoming a trucking entrepreneur is to understand the basics of your business. This chapter will provide some basic information on the business of trucking by defining common terms, exploring different responsibilities, and teaching you the basics of running a business.

Let's start with your business plan, an important piece of document that serves as a north-star for your business and the opportunity for you to share with potential investors your business proposition.

Trucking Business Plan

A business plan is a written document that outlines the particulars of your business, including the mission statement, a breakdown of the team/company structure, a financial projection, and more. The purpose of this document is to outline your business goals and propose solutions to achieve them.

The business plan serves as a guide for execution. Once you have completed the plan, it serves as a tool for you to track your progress, which helps you execute the business plan.

It's important to note that a business plan is not a one-time document. While it is great to outline your goals and strategies in the beginning, it's also vital to review and update your business plan as time goes on.

The primary audience for the business plan includes:

- Investors – Your investors will be reviewing more than just the financial projections in your business plan. They will also want to know about who they are giving their hard-earned money to and how they plan to manage it. This is where your business plan becomes an important part of building credibility with potential investors. It demonstrates that you have sound knowledge of the industry and can lead them to believe that you can make sound decisions on their behalf.
- Employees – As we all know, employees are not only an investment but also an important aspect of your company culture. It is important that employees understand why they are working for their company, how they contribute to its success and how they can grow with it—all of which are outlined in a well-written business plan. This will help them align their career goals with the overall strategy of the company.
- Customers – Ultimately, your customers are your revenue stream. In order to keep them happy and loyal, it is vital to understand their needs and the marketplace. This is why it is important to create a detailed customer profile, including their needs and wants as well as the competition you face.
- Partners – Similar to employees, partners such as suppliers and services providers need an understanding of how they fit into the overall business plan. It's important for them to know that you have a

plan for expansion and future success. A good business plan provides this information in an easy-to-understand format that can be communicated easily with both parties.

A business plan should have the following components:

Executive Summary

The Executive Summary is a high-level overview of your business plan. It should include the key objectives of the business, financial projections, and the overall strategy for achieving each of them. This part of your business plan is typically read by investors, so it should be written in an engaging way that will get them excited about investing in your company.

For example, if you are planning on expanding your fleet of trucks, your Executive Summary should include a description of the fleet you will be working with (make, model, fuel efficiency), the trucks you will be purchasing, as well as a breakdown of projected costs.

Mission Statement

The Mission Statement is typically the first section of the business plan. It provides a general outline of what your company does and why it exists. This part should answer questions such as: Who are you? What do you do? Why do you exist? How does your company contribute to society? How can people benefit from your service? Why will customers choose to do business with you over others in the industry?

For example, "We are a new company that specializes in trucking services. We help to reduce the cost of transporting goods across the country, while providing quality customer service. Our goal is to make it easier for customers to transport their goods from point A to point B by providing a convenient and cost-effective alternative to other transportation companies."

Company Description

The Company Description outlines the structure of your business and how each division works together. It should include an executive summary, which describes your business (size, scope, etc.), as well as a breakdown of departments and/or divisions (Accounting, Sales & Marketing, Operations, HR & Administration). This will provide you with an opportunity to outline how each division contributes to the overall success of your company.

For example: "Our company is a new start-up that specializes in providing trucking services for local businesses. The company was founded as a small business focused on developing long-term relationships with our clients. We have developed innovative processes that make it easy for our clients to transport their products across the country."

Analysis of Market Opportunities

The Analysis of Market Opportunities section outlines the industry trends and market opportunities you are looking at pursuing. This section can also include an analysis of your competition. It should include an overview of the industry, including key challenges and growth areas.

For example: "The trucking industry has seen a decline in profits over the last decade. This is due to a variety of factors, including increased fuel costs, high overhead costs, and more stringent regulations from federal and local authorities. There is a strong need for the trucking industry to evolve with the times in order to remain competitive."

You should also include a breakdown of your industry, including the following:

- Type of goods you are transporting (breakdown by weight, miles, and mode of transport)
- The distribution channels you are working with (wholesalers, retailers, etc.)
- Cost structure for both your client and yourself (breakdown of expenses related to operations, including wages, taxes, fuel costs, and more)
- Key competitors in the space and how you see your company competing with them over the next two to five years. This can also include key suppliers that you work with on a regular basis.

Financial Projections

The Financial Projections should include a detailed breakdown of projected revenue and expenses for the next two to five years. This section can also include a breakdown of key assumptions that will affect your revenue projections (e.g., fuel prices over time). It is important to be as transparent as possible when it comes to financial projections. Avoiding a detailed breakdown here is not only dishonest but also might give investors the impression that you don't have a solid business plan in place. It is always better to be transparent than it is to be deceptive.

Remember: the best way to get someone interested in investing in your company is to demonstrate your ability to manage their money. This means showing them that you understand the business and the industry inside and out as well as demonstrating that you have a plan for growth.

Team/Company Structure

This section of the business plan will outline the structure of your company, including key positions in each division (VP of Operations, Director of Sales & Marketing). It should also include job descriptions for each role and a breakdown of responsibilities. This provides potential investors with an understanding of who they will be working with at your company.

For example: "Our organization is a small team with a lean structure. We have a VP of Operations in charge of day-to-day operations, including hiring, scheduling and managing our fleet of trucks."

Financial Section

The Financial Section is typically broken into two parts. The first part is an overview that includes financial data such as cash flow projections, top-line revenue projections, and expenses related to operations (wages, taxes, fuel costs). The second part is more granular in nature and includes more detailed information on key expenses such as marketing costs, debt payments and other capital expenditures. It should also include forecasts on key financial metrics such as EBITDA (Earnings Before Interest, Taxes, Depreciation, and Amortization) and Net Profit.

For example: "We expect our top-line revenue to increase from $XXX in year 1 to $XXX in year 2 and then increase to $XXX in year 3. In terms of expenses, we expect our Marketing & Sales costs will increase from $YYY in year 1 to $YYY in year 2 and then increase to $YYY by the end of the third year."

What not to include:

There are a few things that you should avoid including when creating your business plan. While it is important to be as transparent as possible, there is information that investors will not need or want to see. This includes the following:

- Financial Data – Unless you are targeting a specific investor (such as a bank), including your financial data is typically unnecessary. It's best to focus on the overall strategy of your company instead of overwhelming readers with numbers that are irrelevant for their investment decision making process. Remember, keep it simple. The objective here is for them to understand the opportunity you are presenting them with—not analyzing every detail in your business model.
- Customer Data – Similar to financial data, including customer data is also not typically necessary. The purpose of the business plan is to present a well-thought-out strategy for your company (not sell your company).

- Confidential Information – While it is important to be transparent with investors, there are some things that they don't need to know. This includes detailed financials of other companies that you are working with (e.g., other businesses you might be partnering with).
- Your Personal Expectations – You should never include your personal expectations in your business plan. This includes salaries, housing arrangements, and other related items. These issues are best left for the negotiation table after the initial investment term has been agreed upon.

The business plan should be easy-to-read and include a combination of text and graphics that provide visual representations of key points. For example, you can include a graphic representation of the team structure or an illustration demonstrating expected revenue growth over time. Be creative here—these visuals will help break up large amounts of information and help readers digest it more easily.

Once you have completed your business plan, it's time to share it with potential investors and other key stakeholders in your business ecosystem.

Why You Should Share Your Business Plan

While some might be hesitant at the idea of sharing their plans for success with others, it can actually have a positive effect on your company's success (as long as you don't share everything).

Sharing a business plan offers potential investors confidence in the decision they will make when choosing whether or not to invest in your business venture. It also helps build credibility among potential partners while helping them feel more invested in your business.

Sometimes, the line between being a business owner and a truck driver can get blurred. Many entrepreneurs are owners who also operate as drivers. However, it's important to understand that there is a difference between them.

Business Owner vs. Truck Driver

While trucking is an essential part of your business, it's important to understand that you are not your drivers. You are responsible for the business and your drivers are responsible for the truck. If there is an issue with a driver, you should not try to fix it yourself, but rather call the driver's manager and let them know what is going on.

The Importance of a Professional Image

In order to build credibility with investors and potential partners, it's important that you have a professional image. This includes everything from your email address to how you dress when visiting partners. The main point here is that you want to look professional.

Having a professional image will go a long way in building credibility for you and your company. That means that even if you work out of your home office or garage, it's important to keep things clean and organized so that people don't think you're just some "fly by night" operation looking for their next big score. This goes hand-in-hand with how others perceive your business, so it matters!

It's not just about how others perceive you but also about how you perceive yourself. It can be tempting to wear jeans and sweatshirts all the time but this can also send a message to others that you don't take your business seriously. That is not the image you want to send to potential investors and partners!

For many entrepreneurs, it can be easy to get caught up in the day-to-day tasks of running a business instead of focusing on the long-term strategy. The key is to create a balance between thinking short term and long term.

Short Term vs. Long Term

While being able to manage your short-term goals and objectives is important, it's also vital that you have a strategy for the long-term success of your business. This includes:

With so much focus on making money and getting things done for the short run, it's easy for companies to lose sight of the bigger picture. However, by creating a strategy for the next 3–5 years, you will be more likely to succeed in building a successful company over time. It allows you to think strategically instead of tactically about how your business will reach its full potential in the future.

The key is to ensure that you have a balance between short-term and long-term goals. Having too much focus on the short term can be just as detrimental to your business as trying to create a long-term strategy without any short-term goals. The trick is to find a balance between the two in order to get your business where you want it to go.

Cash Flow

Cash flow is how much money flows into and out of your business. But, what do you do when the cash stops flowing? Or, what do you do if it keeps flowing and you have so much cash that you can't use it all? Here are some tips to help you better manage your cash flow:

When buying new equipment, always purchase used equipment before financing. This way, if the business isn't profitable, at least you didn't tie up all of your capital in a loan.

Use a credit card for purchases that will take too long to pay off. This way you will be able to pay off larger purchases over time without tying up all of your capital. Just be careful to not charge more than what you can afford to pay back. This will help keep from getting buried in debt.

For example, if you decide to purchase a new truck, go ahead and use your credit card for the down payment. Then, use your cash flow from the profits of your business to pay off the rest of the balance on the truck over time.

Use a line of credit as a last resort. These types of loans are usually easier to get than other types of loans, but you will be charged higher interest rates.

The best rule is to not spend more money than you earn in a given month. This way, you won't get into debt and you won't have to worry about running out of cash.

Taxes

Most trucking businesses are considered "pass-through" entities. This means that the business itself does not pay federal or state taxes; instead, the owner pays taxes on his or her individual income tax return.

You will have to pay income tax on your net earnings from the business and this will either be in the form of a line item on your individual tax return or it will be calculated as an adjustment to your taxable income.

The IRS has made it easier for individual truckers to enter their expenses by providing a Standard Mileage Deduction chart. This allows you to deduct a certain amount based on the distance you drive your truck each year. If you are eligible for this deduction, all you have to do is keep track of your miles and enter them into your tax software.

With tax laws constantly changing, it is important to understand how the changes will affect your business. For example, did you know that the IRS has changed the way it treats meals and lodging?

If meals and lodging are required as a condition of employment for you to be able to work, these expenses may now be deducted from your income. Furthermore, if you pay for meals or lodging on behalf of a family member, these expenses may now be deducted if they are not included in their wages or compensation.

But what about if you buy a Coke from a vending machine? Unfortunately for truckers who spend long hours on the road, food and beverages purchased from vending machines are not considered deductible.

Knowledge is power when it comes to taxes, so spend some time learning the ins and outs of how your business will be taxed.

Tax Year

The tax year is a specific period of time during the year that you use to report your income and expenses for tax purposes. For example, the tax year for most small businesses in the U.S. is January 1 through December 31. If you are an owner-operator, then your tax year may be a calendar year (January 1 through December 31 of every year) or it may be a fiscal year (for example, July 1 through June 30 of the next calendar year).

No matter which tax year you choose, it will apply to all aspects of your business—including accounting, payroll and income taxes. So, if you use a fiscal tax year, then all of your accounting records must be prepared as if they were for those 12 months, which encompasses the entire time period of actual business activity. For example, if your fiscal tax year is July 1st through June 30th (called "periods" in accounting), then you will need to adjust all of your accounts on January 1st. This means that you will need to make appropriate adjustments depending on the accounting method you use. In addition, certain firms or individual taxpayers may choose to adopt a 52-week or 53-week fiscal year instead of the standard 12 months.

The most common tax year for a small business is the calendar tax year which means that the accounting records should include the entire business activity of 12 months. This makes it easy because there is only one set of books and there are no periods or adjusting required on January 1 (or any other time). As a result, this option creates less work and fewer headaches for the trucking entrepreneur—and so we recommend it.

Record Filing

An important part of running a business is maintaining accurate records. This means keeping good track of your income and expenses, as well as understanding the financial health of your business.

The trucking industry is highly regulated so you will need to keep certain records on file with the Federal Motor Carrier Safety Administration (FMCSA) and/or the Department of Transportation (DOT). Some examples include:

Driver's logbook – This logbook maintains the records of your hours of service. It is important that this be kept meticulously because it is used by FMCSA to determine violations and penalties.

Driver qualification files – These files are used to keep track of any medical or physical problems associated with drivers, including their diagnosis, treatment, medications taken, or restrictions imposed by a doctor. In other words, if a driver has a problem that could affect his ability to drive safely, these files are what's used to prove it.

Vehicle records – These records include the VIN number, purchase date, and transfer information about the trucks used for business. If your business uses a leased or rented fleet, you will also need to keep track of the VIN numbers on those vehicles as well.

Other important records include:

Driver hiring files – This file includes medical certificates and other documents that are used to verify that the driver is medically qualified to drive a commercial vehicle.

Record retention – This is what you use to keep track of your business's income and expenses over time for tax purposes.

Accounting

Accounting is an important function of all businesses. It is the system that tracks the financial health of a company, and it is used to prepare financial statements and tax returns. Accounting involves collecting, recording, analyzing, and reporting financial transactions.

It is important to understand that accounting isn't just about numbers; it's about recording business transactions in a way that helps you understand the true financial health of your business. This allows you to make better decisions for your business—whether they are short-term decisions or long-term decisions.

For example, you may have a good idea about how much money you are losing on a particular route because you have been tracking your miles and expenses while on that route. However, if you don't know what the average mileage for that route is, or if you don't know the expense breakdown of that route, then you can't truly understand what's happening with that particular route.

In general terms, there are two main categories of accounting:

1. Financial Accounting, which is required by banks and government agencies for tax purposes. This type of accounting is used to report net income (profit) to shareholders as well as the IRS.
2. Management Accounting, which is used for internal management decisions—like setting prices and evaluating new investments in equipment or vehicles. This type of accounting allows managers to make better business decisions based on their company's financial condition and market environment. It also makes it easier for managers to compare their performance with other firms in their industry.

There are at least two ways to prepare accounting statements:

1. cash basis accounting; or
2. accrual basis accounting.

The method chosen will depend on your business structure and your choice of tax year (more information below). If you decide not to have an accountant prepare your accounting records, then you will need to understand the difference between cash basis and accrual basis accounting so that you can do it yourself.

Cash Accounting

Cash accounting is the easiest type of accounting. It simply means that the business only records transactions when money actually changes hands. For example, if you sell a truck for $10,000 but don't receive payment for 30 days, then this transaction is not recorded until you have received the money—even though you have already sold the truck. The advantage is that this method is very simple and easy to understand, but it isn't always useful in making decisions about your business because there isn't a connection between revenue (receipts) and expenses (payments).

Accrual Accounting

Accrual accounting records transactions when they take place, regardless of whether or not money has actually changed hands. So if you sell a truck for $10,000 but don't receive payment for 30 days, then this transaction is recorded and counted as revenue when it takes place (even though no money has changed hands yet). The advantage with using accrual accounting is that it will allow you to make better financial decisions about your business because there is a direct connection between revenue and expenses. However, this method is more complicated to understand and it is more time-consuming to prepare the accounting records.

If you decide to use a calendar tax year, then you will need to change your accounting records every year when you file your taxes. This means that you will need to adjust all of your accounts on April 15 (or whatever date is used in your country) even though that is the first day of your new tax year. This means that you will need to make adjustments (called "periods" in accounting) for each month from January through March. If this sounds confusing, it is—so it's best not to mess with this option.

Financial Statements

Financial statements are summaries of the financial information from a business or individual. There are three common types of financial statements:

1. income statement;
2. balance sheet; and
3. cash flow statement.

The income statement summarizes sales revenue and expenses for a period of time—usually one month, one quarter, or one year. It shows how much money was brought into the business (sales revenue), how much was spent (expenses), and how much money was left over (profit).

A balance sheet summarizes your assets (property, equipment, inventory, etc.), your liabilities (debts), and your equity (owner's investment). It also shows the difference between the two—which is called stockholder's equity. So if you have $25,000 in assets, $5,000 in debts and $20,000 in stockholder's equity—then you would have a net worth of $20,000. The advantage with a balance sheet is that it allows you to see how much money you've invested and how much money you have left to work with.

A cash flow statement summarizes how much cash has come into your business or household and how much cash has been paid out over a period of time. It usually includes income statements as well as variations on the balance sheet. For example, instead of listing "cash" under assets—it may list "checking account" or "savings account." Instead of listing "debt" under liabilities—it may list "credit card balances" or "car loan." This allows for more detail on where the cash comes from and where it goes.

Budgeting

Budgeting is simply planning for the future. There are three basic budgets:

1. operating budget;
2. capital budget; and
3. cash flow budget.

Operating Budget

An operating budget forecasts sales revenue, expenses, and profits for a set time period—usually one month or one quarter. This is also known as a "profit and loss" budget. It is basically an income statement that is extended out over time. Most businesses have monthly operating budgets, but some have quarterly or annual operating budgets as well.

Capital Budget

A capital budget forecasts the purchase of major assets like land, buildings, equipment, and vehicles for a set time period—usually one year or less. This can also be called an "investment" or "capital expenditure" budget.

Capital budgets are especially important when you own your own business because your growth will be limited by your available capital. A typical small business will spend most of its capital on vehicles and buildings over its lifetime so these purchases should be planned carefully—just like the purchase of a new car would be planned carefully by an individual family member.

All too often, people buy new equipment without first doing adequate research on prices, reliability, safety features, and other factors to ensure that they are getting the best value for their money.

Cash Flow Budget

A cash flow budget forecasts how much cash will come into your business or household and how much cash will go out over a set period of time. This is also called a "budgeted income statement" because it is an income statement that is extended out over time. Cash flow budgets are especially important for businesses because they allow you to see how much money you will have available to pay your expenses at different times of the year. Businesses can get into a lot of financial trouble if they do not understand their seasonal sales patterns and do not plan accordingly for their peaks and valleys.

For example, a lawn service may make most of its revenue during the summer months so it needs to plan accordingly for these seasonal increases in revenue. A trucking business may see a significant increase in revenue during the winter months due to an increase in demand for shipping and therefore should plan accordingly to make sure it has enough drivers available during this peak period of activity.

An important part of seasonal planning is forecasting when you will be making investments—such as purchasing new equipment or hiring additional drivers—so that you can make sure that you have enough working capital available when you need it.

There are several basic types of budgets:

1. zero-based budgeting;
2. modified zero-based budgeting;
3. objectives-based budgeting; and
4. activity-based budgeting.

Zero-Based Budgeting

Zero-based budgeting is a technique pioneered by Silicon Valley computer chip maker, Intel Corporation. Zero-based budgeting is similar to the "modified zero-based" and "objectives based" techniques.

It requires a company to examine all of its activities and costs and eliminate those that are not absolutely necessary for the survival of the company. This technique requires that all expenses be identified—regardless of how much was spent on that item in previous years—and then each expense needs to be justified for each upcoming year.

In other words, if you had spent $100,000 on salaries last year, you cannot simply plan on spending more than $100,000 this year unless you have specific reasons for increasing your employee's salaries. Zero based budgets can be especially useful for businesses that have been losing money or not making enough money to support their cost structure— because it forces them to look critically at expenses, they may have previously considered non-negotiable.

Modified Zero-Based Budgets

Modified zero based budgets require that all expenses be justified as was previously described in the "zero based" budgeting technique. However, modified zero based budgets allow past expenses to be carried forward for a period of time. For example, if you had $100,000 in salaries last year and this year your salaries are just $90,000—then you will need to find a way to cut back on your payroll costs.

If you had been making $100,000 per year for the past three years and were planning on keeping your payroll at that level for the next three years—then you would have an easier time justifying your spending to upper management. In other words, zero based budgets force everyone to be more frugal with expenses—but modified zero based budgets allow a business to maintain some of its long-term spending commitments when it is appropriate.

Objectives-Based Budgeting

Objectives-based budgeting is a technique pioneered by the U.S. Department of Defense that relies on objectives (goals) instead of figures (numbers). This technique allows managers from different departments within an organization to set their own goals without having to plan how they will achieve those goals or how much money will be spent achieving those goals.

This is called "bottom up" planning because it starts from the bottom of the organization and works its way up.

For example, if an employee wants to improve her sales performance by 20%, then she will need to come up with a plan of how she will achieve this goal. She may decide to hire additional salespeople or increase the amount of advertising and public relations for her products. She would then submit a proposal to her supervisor and ask for the necessary funds to spend on these activities.

This technique is especially useful when dealing with intangible goals—such as increased quality control or improved customer satisfaction—because it is hard to measure improvements in these areas with a simple "yes" or "no."

Activity-Based Budgets

Activity-based budgets are often called "balanced scorecards" because they can incorporate all four budgeting techniques into one format. A balanced scorecard includes both financial and non-financial information in order to provide a more complete view of the business goals and objectives.

This format takes advantage of the strengths of each budgeting technique: zero-based budgets provide a clear picture of expenses, modified zero-based budgets give you some ability to carry forward past expenses, objectives-based budgets allow you to set your own goals and activity-based budgets give you some flexibility in measuring your progress. An activity-based budget will often contain all four formats within one document.

Pricing

Pricing is the method of determining how much you will charge your customers for your goods or services. There are two basic methods of pricing: cost-plus pricing and market-based pricing.

Cost-plus Pricing

Cost-plus pricing is the most common method of pricing because it's easier to implement. It simply adds a markup (cost plus) to the actual cost of goods sold or services provided. For example, if you purchase a good for $1 and sell it for $2, then you have a 100% markup (or margin).

Market-based Pricing

Market-based pricing is more difficult to implement because it requires you to determine what your competitors charge for similar products or services and then try to undercut them while still turning a profit.

For example, if competitor A charges $3 for an apple and competitor B charges $5, then competitor A would be using market-based pricing. Not only do they want a profit—but they also want to make sure that their price is lower than competitor B's price so that more people will buy from them instead of from competitor B.

However, if both competitors A and B are charging the same amount ($5)—then they are using either cost-plus or competitive bidding.

Pricing has always been one of the most important factors in the success of a small business. If your price is too high, your customers will go elsewhere. If it's too low, you won't be able to pay your bills. The trick is to determine what customers are willing to pay for your goods or services and then charge that amount.

Payments

Get Paid

There are several ways your business can get paid.

The most common way your business will get paid is through a check or electronic deposit. However, if you are paying for services or deliveries, you may be required to pay in full before the service is provided. You may also be asked to prepay for a service or delivery—especially if it's a large order.

Another option is credit card payment through services like Square or PayPal. This allows you to accept credit cards and receive an electronic deposit into your bank account more quickly. Credit card payments are also more secure than cash payments because they require an electronic signature rather than an exchange of goods or services for money.

Make Payments

If you are using contracted services, most trucking businesses will need some sort of credit arrangement with the company providing the service. For example, if your truck needs repairs and you have an extended warranty, then you will need some form of financing from the repair shop. If you are paying cash for supplies, then it's likely that you will need to pay them on time, with interest for late fees.

If your business has employees, then payroll taxes and benefits are another important part of payments made by the business itself. Payroll taxes include Social Security and Medicare taxes (FICA) and unemployment taxes. If you have employees, then payroll taxes are mandatory and must be paid regularly.

Liability Insurance

Liability insurance is a type of coverage that protects you from legal responsibility for injuries and property damage caused by your business or operations. There are some basic types of liability insurance, but some business owners buy additional coverage, such as product liability or commercial auto coverage. The following are the most common types of liability insurance:

1. general liability insurance/business owner's policy (BOP);
2. professional liability insurance;
3. product liability insurance; and
4. commercial auto coverage.

General Liability Insurance/Business Owner's Policy (BOP)

This insurance covers accidents that occur on your property or as a result of your business operations. An example of this would be if you had a grease fire in the kitchen, an employee was bitten by a dog at a customer's home, or someone slipped and fell on ice on your property.

This type of insurance combines general and professional liability insurance in one policy. It is designed for sole proprietors or small businesses owners who operate as a limited liability company (LLC) or corporation. It is also known as "errors and omissions" (E&O). The advantage of this type of policy is that it saves money because you don't have to buy two policies. You just have to pay higher premiums because the insurance company is taking on more risk.

Professional Liability Insurance

This insurance covers errors made by you or your employees while conducting professional services for clients. An example of this would be if you accidentally injured someone while performing surgery, negligently caused damage to someone's property, or lost someone's valuables.

Product Liability Insurance

This type of insurance covers injuries caused by faulty products manufactured, distributed, or sold by your business. It also covers injuries caused by products you install on vehicles. To illustrate this point, let's say that you installed a fuel tank cover on a pickup truck for a customer and it leaked gasoline and caught fire. This would be covered under product liability insurance because the truck now has a faulty fuel tank that needs to be replaced. The same thing would hold true if the fuel tank cover was installed improperly and caused an accident.

If your business uses a vehicle for most of its operations, you should consider buying commercial auto coverage. It covers bodily injury and property damage caused by your operation of the vehicle, or by your employees operating the vehicle, or by someone riding in the vehicle with your permission. Commercial auto coverage is similar to regular auto insurance except that it has exclusions such as medical payments coverage and personal injury protection (PIP). These exclusions can be added to the policy if desired by contacting the agent who sold you the policy.

Insurance is not required by law, but it is highly recommended. You may be sued and held liable for your actions or inactions if you buy insurance. For example, if you don't have liability insurance and someone slips and falls on your property, they may sue you and win a judgment for their injuries. If you don't have money to pay the judgment, your personal assets can be seized to pay this debt.

Dispute Resolution

Dispute resolution is the process of settling disagreements between parties who are involved in a dispute. Dispute resolution can be accomplished through mediation, arbitration, and litigation. Some dispute resolutions that you may have heard of include the following:

Mediation

Mediation is a process in which an impartial third party helps two or more people resolve a dispute. The mediator does not take sides and simply facilitates dialogue between the disputing parties. The mediator may also suggest questions for the disputing parties to ask each other that help bring out information that will help them resolve their own dispute.

Arbitration

Arbitration is typically used to settle labor/management disputes and involves an impartial third party (an arbitrator) who listens to both sides of the story and then makes a decision on how to settle the dispute. In arbitration, there are no lawyers, no jury and no witnesses—just one arbitrator. The arbitrator's decision can be based on law or it can be based on what they think is fair under the circumstances. An arbitrator's decision cannot be appealed in an arbitration situation—so once you agree to arbitration as your method of dispute resolution, you give up your right to have your dispute heard by a jury.

Litigation

Litigation occurs when one side of a dispute files a lawsuit against the other party to resolve the dispute. Each side of the lawsuit has an attorney who represents them in court. Witnesses are called, evidence is presented, and legal arguments are made by each side to prove that they are right. In litigation, both sides have a say in how the case is handled and decisions cannot be imposed upon them by any third party—it's their dispute and they fight it out in court.

Negotiation

Negotiation is an attempt to settle a dispute without involving any third party (mediator, arbitrator, or judge). Both parties discuss their positions with each other and come up with their own solution for resolving the dispute. If you can't settle on your own, you may want to hire a professional mediator/arbitrator/judge to help you negotiate an agreement that will work for both of you. Some people don't believe in using outside help when negotiating—but experienced negotiators know that sometimes it's easier to reach agreement with an unbiased mediator who can steer discussions back toward compromise rather than waiting until emotions have cooled and then trying to remember what both parties already agreed to.

For your trucking business, negotiation is one of the most important skills you can learn. You will continually negotiate with your customers, your vendors, and your employees. If you can learn to negotiate effectively, you will find it much easier to get what you want from others and avoid costly disputes.

There are three basic skills involved in any negotiation:

1. preparation;
2. active listening; and
3. objectives.

Preparation

You need to prepare yourself for every negotiation so that you can achieve your objectives. The more time and effort that you put into preparation, the better your chances are of achieving what you want from the negotiation. If possible, try to do some research on the other party so that you have some idea of their interests and objectives before meeting with them for a negotiation. Then use this information to tailor your own objectives and strategy in order to reach an agreement that both parties can live with.

For example, if you are negotiating with a supplier for a lower price on a load of fuel, you may want to find out the supplier's current budget for fuel so that you can figure out if they have money to spend on the extra load of fuel you are trying to purchase. If they don't have any extra money, your objective is much different than if they do have the money available. In the first case, your objective would be to get them to spend their limited supply of money on your extra load. In the second case, your objective would be to get them to set aside some money in their budget for you so that they don't use it for other purposes.

Active Listening

In order to negotiate effectively, you need to understand what the other party is trying to achieve and why they want it. This can be done by active listening—which means listening closely and asking questions when necessary in order to understand what is being said. For example, if someone tells you that their goal is "to make more money," then you may need a follow-up question such as "so how much more do you want?" Or if someone wants "a fair wage," then a follow-up question might be "so what is fair for someone with your experience?"

Active listening is more than just saying "yes" and "I understand"—it's being actively engaged in the conversation so that you fully understand what the other party is trying to achieve.

After listening, you can set your objectives for the negotiation. Your objective should be something that you want from the other party. In other words, your objective should be something that you will say "yes" to if they agree to it. For example, if your objective is "to make more money," then they will probably give you a counter-offer of a higher price for your load of fuel. If your objective was "to get a fair wage," then they may offer you a higher wage but not a fair wage (because they don't know what fair means).

So if you haven't set clear objectives before negotiating—then it's possible that they will offer something that isn't acceptable to you and then neither of you will ever get what you want from the negotiation and no agreement will ever be reached. Once you have decided what your objective is, write it down in order to keep it clear in your mind throughout the negotiation. If you are negotiating with someone over the phone, read your objective to keep it fresh in your mind while you negotiate.

Workplace Safety Issues

Workplace safety is a broad term that describes the precautions taken to ensure the safety of employees. In the trucking industry, workplace safety applies to both drivers and employees who work for the company. In order to prevent on-the-job injuries and fatalities, it is important for employers to take a proactive approach toward safety. The following are some tips for creating a safer work environment:

Provide Safety Training

Training workers on how to safely operate various machines and equipment will reduce the number of workplace injuries. Safety training should be provided before allowing workers to operate machinery or drive trucks. Many drivers are required to undergo regular training under federal guidelines set by the Federal Motor Carrier Safety Administration (FMCSA).

For example, the FMCSA requires drivers to take a Basic Safety Training course. The training consists of two modules (23 hours total) that cover vehicle dynamics, defensive driving techniques, hazardous materials, and driver's license requirements.

Ensure Employee Compliance with Safety Procedures

In addition to ensuring that employees are trained on how to operate equipment safely, it is important to ensure that employees follow these safety procedures every time they operate equipment. For example, some companies have a "three-pronged approach" where an employee has three chances to follow proper safety procedures before being reprimanded and/or fired.

Create a Safer Work Environment

Employers can help create a safer work environment by making sure that machines and equipment are properly maintained. For example, if an employee is injured because of poorly maintained machinery or unsafe operating conditions, the company may be found liable for the injury. It is also important to maintain a safe driving environment by ensuring that your fleet is outfitted with properly functioning seat belts and other necessary protective devices such as airbags and roll bars.

In cases where employers have not taken the necessary steps to protect their workers from injury, the courts may award compensation for lost wages or medical bills through a workers' compensation claim.

It is important to note that a worker does not have to be injured or killed for a workplace safety claim to be valid. Even if an employee is not injured directly, he or she may still have grounds for a personal injury lawsuit if the employer's negligence has caused others to be injured or killed.

For example, a truck driver's company may have required him to drive faster than the speed limit in order to make his next delivery on time. This may cause him to get into an accident with another vehicle on the road. Even though this truck driver was not hurt in the accident, he would still have grounds for a personal injury lawsuit against his employer because the company forced him to risk his safety by driving at unsafe speeds.

The issue of workplace safety does not apply only to truck drivers and employees. It also applies to the general public. For example, a trucking company may require its drivers to travel at unsafe speeds in order to meet a deadline. This may cause the driver to get into an accident with another vehicle on the road. In this case, the other driver would have grounds for a personal injury lawsuit against the trucking company because they were operating their truck in an unsafe manner that resulted in injury to a member of the public.

Chapter 4: Operating Strategies

The operating strategies for an owner-operator trucking business are what separates the men from the boys. In this chapter, I'll outline some of the operating strategies that have worked for me in my own trucking business.

I'll make no bones about it; my operating strategies are very aggressive, and you may not be comfortable with them at first. But as you will see, they do work if they're applied correctly.

You don't have to agree with me on every point. As a matter of fact, I sure hope you don't agree with me on every point! Otherwise, I'm not doing my job properly! What I am trying to do is present a different perspective on things—a perspective that has worked for me personally when it comes to running a successful business. This chapter is offered in that spirit.

Types of Trucks

The Straight Truck

The straight truck is the most common type of heavy truck used by owner operators. A straight truck looks like a box on wheels, and is primarily used to haul freight across the country. Straight trucks are usually owned by big fleets and leased to owner-operators.

The Step Deck

The step deck is a modified version of the straight truck that has been designed to maximize the cube space on the trailer. By having a raised deck—a "step"—on top of the cab, more cargo can be loaded onto the trailer than would normally be possible with a normal straight truck. Step decks are usually owned by small fleets that lease their trucks to owner-operators.

The Van

The van is essentially a box on wheels, just like a straight truck, but it's smaller in size and is typically used for local hauling within a city or state rather than across the country. Vans are usually owned by small independent companies that lease them to owner-operators.

Your choice of what kind of truck you'll drive is ultimately up to you; however, I recommend that new drivers start out with either a step deck or van (vans are easier because they're smaller and cheaper to operate). This is because for new drivers, the vast majority of their hauls will involve local hauling. In fact, for most new drivers, hauling within a state or two will be the norm.

Semi-Truck

The semi-truck is a huge, heavy truck designed to carry freight across the country. I recommend that new owner operators avoid semi-trucks at first, because they are more expensive to operate than straight trucks or vans.

When you're first starting out, your goal should be to make as much money as possible with the smallest amount of risk possible. While it's true that semi-trucks are more profitable on a mile-per-mile basis than smaller trucks, they're also riskier. The reason for this is that an inexperienced driver can't handle a semi-truck nearly as well as he can handle a straight truck or van. And if you get into an accident in a semi-truck, you'll probably get fired and lose your CDL!

In addition, an inexperienced driver can't load and unload his own trailer nearly as quickly in a semi-truck compared to a straight or step deck, which means he'll spend more time standing around waiting for customers to arrive or for his trailer to get loaded and unloaded. This results in lost income.

Trailer Acquisition

One of the most important operating strategies you can employ is to buy a trailer that will work best for your business.

By that, I mean, go out and find a trailer that you never have to worry about. Find a trailer that will hold up to the environment in which it will be used. Find a trailer with parts and components that are readily available and easy to install. And find one with an overall design that gives you a lot of flexibility and versatility when it comes to what you can haul in it.

In other words, don't settle for second best when it comes to purchasing trailers for your trucking company. It's not worth the headaches!

Many new truckers start out with what I call "trailer trash." They get handed down trailers from friends or family members or they purchase cheapo trailers from auctions or online sources such as eBay. It doesn't take long until these trailers are well past their prime and quickly on their way to being derelict and useless. Some of my clients have even found skunks living inside their trucks!

Skunks! Not an uncommon sight inside your average used trucking equipment!

Consider this: if you buy a cheap $5,000 trailer that has to be repaired every year, and those repairs cost another $5,000, you're losing money! And you're also losing time—both in the shop and on the road. If you lose time on the road, your profits will decline as well.

The small cost of a trailer that will stand the test of time is worth it! Take it from me. I've bought some trailers in my day, and I've wasted a lot of money on junk too. It's not fun to buy a trailer and then ship it back to the seller for a refund!

So, don't be afraid to spend $10,000 or $15,000 on your first trailer. As your business grows, you'll have no regrets about doing so!

I recommend you start out with at least two trailers: one flatbed (which can be used for all sorts of different jobs) and one refrigerated trailer (which can be used for transporting just about anything). If you can afford more than two, by all means buy them! The more trailers you have available, the more flexibility you will have in choosing what type of loads to haul. That flexibility is key when running a successful business.

There are different acquisition strategies you might want to consider as well. For example, I know one guy who purchased his first two trailers from a local dealership instead of from a private party. The dealer was able to give him a couple of good deals on the trailers, and he still had plenty of money left over to fix them up and modify them to fit his needs.

Another strategy is to purchase your trailers from an existing trucking company that's going out of business. Many times, these companies have trailers that are in good shape but need some minor modifications in order to make them work for your specific purposes. You can also sometimes get a good deal on their other equipment such as refrigeration units and generators.

I know several other truckers who started out with nothing but used equipment, including trailers. They bought it all at auctions or online sources such as eBay or Craigslist. And they've had great success with their businesses!

So, don't worry about what others may think when you buy used equipment for your trucking company. If it works for them, it will work for you too! And if you do run into issues with used equipment, there are always ways to fix those issues that don't involve buying new equipment.

In some cases, you can purchase used equipment and make it look and function like new again! This is especially true for older trailers that haven't been abused.

I purchased a used trailer that was built in the late 1980s, and I had it looking like new in a matter of months! That included adding all new lights, adding a tailgate, and painting the whole thing (including the frame). It worked perfectly and held up to the test of time as well! I couldn't have purchased an all-new trailer for what it cost me to refurbish that one. And in this case, I got a much better deal!

Types of Trailers

There are many different types of trailers that you can purchase to use in your own trucking business. Each of these is designed for a specific purpose, and you will need to learn about the different types and what they are used for in order to determine which type of trailer would be best suited for your particular needs. Here are some of the most common types of trailers that you may encounter:

Flatbed

This is one of the most common types of trailers available. It has a flat platform at the back and is typically used for hauling large, heavy items that won't fit in a regular trailer. These items can include machinery and other bulky items that need to be shipped across the country. Flatbed trailers can vary in length, but the most common size is around 40 feet in length.

For example, if you are hauling a large piece of machinery, you will need a flatbed trailer to haul it on. A regular trailer may not be able to hold the weight of the machinery, so if you are going to be hauling heavy items that won't fit in a normal trailer, a flatbed is your best option.

Dump Trailer

A dump trailer is very similar to a flatbed but is used for carrying dirt and other heavy materials that can't be dumped by hand. This type of trailer is equipped with hydraulic arms that are controlled from inside the cab; these arms can be raised and lowered as needed to help dump the load.

These trailers typically have a large box at the back where you can place dirt or other materials that you will then dump onto some sort of land fill when you arrive at your destination. These trailers can also be used for carrying other types of materials, such as sand or gravel, depending on what your needs are. Dump trailers can vary in length, but they typically range between 18-28 feet long.

V-Nose Trailer

A v-nose trailer, sometimes called an angle-nose or visor nose trailer, is slightly different from the other types of trailers. This is because the nose of the trailer is angled in such a way that it will point toward the back instead of the front. These trailers are used for hauling oversized loads that won't fit in a normal box trailer. They can be from 40-60 feet long, and while they are typically wider than a standard box trailer, they don't have a flatbed, so you won't be able to haul very large items with this type of trailer.

Cargo Trailer

A cargo trailer is a standard sized box trailer that is used to haul just about any type of cargo, from furniture to construction materials to household items. These trailers can vary in length depending on what type of cargo you will be moving with them. You can also choose between two types: straight deck or drop deck. A straight deck has no sides or walls and is typically used for short distance hauls where you don't have to worry about loading or unloading things out of the trailer yourself; it's more like an extra-long pickup truck bed than an actual trucking trailer. A drop deck, on the other hand, has walls and can be loaded from within using a ramp in order to load and unload cargo.

If you are going to be hauling a lot of different types of cargo, it's best to get a standard cargo trailer. This way you can use it for most jobs and can haul the type of items that you need. You may also want to consider getting a drop deck if you will be loading your trailer yourself; this way, you don't have to worry about driving in and out of places with the ramp down. With a drop deck, you can load items into the trailer yourself and then simply drive out of your garage or driveway without worrying about setting up the ramp again for the next load.

Tank Trailer

A tank trailer is designed to carry liquid products in large tanks that are typically between 4,000-4,200 gallons in size. The tanks will be located inside the trailer itself, so they need to be able to hold up under pressure without leaking or breaking open. Tank trailers also must have special ventilation systems installed on them so that there is enough oxygen inside for fuel vapors to not build up inside the tanks while they are being transported. Tank trailers come in all different sizes depending on what type of liquid product you will be hauling; these sizes range from 32-60 feet in length.

Dry Van Trailer

A dry van trailer is a standard box trailer that can be used for hauling a variety of different types of goods. These trailers can vary in length, and you will typically be able to load them from inside the trailer using a ramp. Although these trailers are commonly used to haul dry goods such as food, building materials, clothing, and other non-liquid products, you can also use them to haul liquid products such as gasoline or chemicals if you are hauling them from one location to another.

Refrigerated Van Trailer

A refrigerated van trailer is a special type of trailer that is designed for hauling perishable items that need to remain cold or frozen during transport. These trailers come in all different sizes depending on what types of items you will be carrying; they usually have insulated walls inside the trailer that can keep the cargo cool or frozen during transport. The trailers will have special vents along the side of the trailer that will allow the cool air to circulate inside the trailer. These trailers can also be equipped with an electric refrigeration unit that will help keep the cargo frozen during transport.

Buying or Leasing

Leasing a truck can be a great way to get started in the business, but you should always consider purchasing your own truck.

This is especially true if you plan on doing this for years to come.

If you are buying a new truck every two years or so, it is not hard to find the monthly payments to be very expensive. If you purchase your own truck when you are starting out, you can take advantage of lower payments and terms that are available for first time buyers.

You should go through every option for leasing and financing before making a decision on how to purchase your truck. This will ensure that you have all the facts and the best possible deal.

Here are some considerations when buying or leasing:

Purchase a New vs. Used Truck

Even though you will have to finance the purchase of a new truck, it can be a great investment. You will have a truck that has many more years of service life ahead of it.

If your business is successful, you will most likely be able to sell the truck within a couple of years and have a net profit. It is probably not worth it to buy a new truck if your business will only last for a short period of time.

Used trucks can be much less expensive, but you may be stuck with the payments and repairs if you do not sell it before the payments are due.

Test Drive

Test driving is an important part of buying any vehicle. If you have never driven a truck before, test driving it can give you valuable information on how easy or difficult it will be for you to drive. This can also give you information on how easy or difficult it may be to pass the driving part of your CDL exam. Test driving the used trucks for sale in your area should give you an idea as to how they are priced in relation to their condition, and how far they have been driven if they were previously used for other purposes such as construction or delivery (U-Haul). You can also get an idea of whether or not they are well maintained by checking their oil, tire, and fluid levels.

Condition and Maintenance

When you are buying a used truck, take the time to inspect it thoroughly for any signs of damage or rust. Also make sure the engine has been maintained. If you have a problem with the engine, it can be very expensive to fix. Also make sure that maintenance records are available if you plan on buying a used truck. This can be very important in helping to avoid problems later on. You should also make sure the truck is in good shape mechanically before test driving it. If there are any problems that need to be fixed before you take delivery of the vehicle, this should be done prior to purchase so you will not have any unexpected surprises once you own it.

Inspect all major components such as the engine, transmission, brakes, tires, etc., when test driving a used truck for sale for potential purchase. Make sure that they are in good condition and ready for safe operation. If anything needs fixing or replacing prior to purchase, get this work done prior to taking delivery of your new vehicle so that there will not be any surprises later on.

The most common issues with used trucks are:

Leaks: Look for oil leaks and signs that the truck has been in an accident. Check under the engine and around the frame rails to look for signs of damage. Also look for rust in the frame rails and body panels. This can be very expensive to repair.

Brakes: If you are going to be hauling heavy loads, make sure the brakes work properly and will be capable of stopping your truck when needed. If they need replacing, have them done before taking delivery of your truck so you will not have any surprises once you own it.

Tires: Check all four tires for condition, tread depth, and tread wear patterns on a used truck for sale before making a purchase decision. Make sure there is enough tread remaining to safely carry a load (1/8" or more). This may require replacing some or all of the tires if you plan on using it as an owner-operator or will be hauling heavy loads such as furniture or construction materials. You should also check tire pressure and rotate every 5,000 miles to help extend their life span and improve fuel economy. You should carry this out yourself at least once every six months by checking with your local tire dealer to see if they have a rotating machine. If they don't, they should be able to tell you where there are tire dealers in your area that do. You should also keep a tire gauge in the truck at all times for easy access when checking the pressure on the tires.

Tires are one of the most important parts of your truck. They can make or break your business. If you take care of them, they will take care of you and give you years of safe operation. Make sure they are in good condition before test driving your potential purchase so there will not be any surprises later on.

The cost of tires is usually low enough to pay for itself several times over when it comes to safety and avoiding costly repairs to other components if you had a blow out or other tire related problem while hauling heavy loads.

Other Components: Make sure all the other components such as fuel lines are in good condition and will not leak under pressure or cause damage or problems once you own this used truck for sale. Check components such as air conditioning, windshield wipers, wipers, mirrors, door locks, seats, steering wheel, etc., for condition before test driving so there will not be any surprises later on.

Financing

You should always check out the financing options and rates available before deciding to buy or lease a truck. You may be able to get lower payments on a new truck if you can find a good rate.

You may also be able to get a lower interest rate if you have good credit. Rates are usually lower for first time buyers with good credit. This can save you a lot of money over the life of the loan.

There are many different types of financing available for trucks and other vehicles such as:

Credit unions, banks, manufacturers, fleet companies, financing companies, leasing companies, and others. You should check out all the options available in your area before deciding on how to finance the purchase of your new truck or used vehicle. There can be substantial differences in the rates and terms available from one company to another. This can make a big difference in how much money it will cost you overall.

Financing Options

Financing options are available for almost any type of business, and you should check out all the options available to you. Get as many quotes as possible so that you can compare rates and terms between the different financing companies. Discuss each of your options with a professional who can help you decide what is best for your situation. There are many good financing companies out there that can help you if you have poor credit. If you have good credit, it can be much easier to get a loan for a new or used truck.

You should always check with the Internal Revenue Service (IRS) for information on how to deduct truck payments from your income taxes. This will help reduce the amount of money that is deducted from your paycheck each month to pay off the loan. You will also be able to deduct certain other expenses such as fuel, repairs, etc., which are related to your truck business when filing your taxes each year. Keep all records such as receipts and invoices in case you are audited by the IRS or state tax authorities.

Credit

If it is possible, it may be beneficial to use one of the following ways to establish good credit before buying a larger vehicle such as a truck:

Buy a small used car and make the monthly payments on time, and eventually pay it off. After you have proven that you are responsible financially, you will be better able to get a lower interest rate on a truck loan.

Check out the credit union in your area. They may have a loan program that they can set up for their members with bad credit, or one that is designed for people who want to establish good credit. Contact them for more information or go online to find out what they can do for you.

Contact your bank or credit union and find out if they offer small loans such as $500 - $1,000 for establishing good credit. If they do, ask about their rates and terms. It may be possible to get a slightly better interest rate than you would with a larger loan from another company. This may also help build your business credit if you make small payments on time each month until the debt is paid off. You should always pay more than the minimum payment due each month so that it will not take too long to pay off the loan (which increases the amount of interest paid). Also make sure you keep copies of all receipts and invoices in case there is ever an IRS audit.

How Much to Finance

The amount you should finance will depend on many factors such as your experience, the truck you buy, and what kind of expenses you have in setting up your business. One advantage to leasing is that it may allow you to purchase a used truck for less money than if you were to finance it with a bank or other financing company. You may also be able to get a lower interest rate when leasing than when financing. If your credit history is good and there is no reason to believe that it will not continue this way, you may be able to secure a loan for the purchase of a new truck if this is how you want to go.

Financing Options

There are many options available for financing your truck purchase or lease. Be sure to compare rates and terms between all the different companies that offer loans or leases on trucks before deciding which one would be best for your situation. Make sure that they can help provide financing for new or used trucks in your area, otherwise they won't be able to help you obtain financing once you find the right vehicle. Some local dealers may also offer their own loan programs for financing trucks that they sell. They can also help by providing advice and suggestions on how to finance your purchase.

Checking out potential used trucks for sale in your area can give you a better idea as to what to expect when purchasing your own truck. You may be able to find some great deals on used trucks for sale if they are in good condition and have been well maintained. Vehicles that have not been maintained can be very costly to repair once you own them if they break down or cause damage to other components. So make sure they are in good condition before test driving, and get the appropriate work done before taking delivery of your new truck so there will not be any surprises once you own it.

Fuel Savings

Fuel is one of the biggest expenses of a trucking business. It is easy to see why when you look at the costs. Fuel costs can quickly get out of hand. If fuel prices go up, so do your truck's fuel bills. Not only that, but long-haul trucks can spend a good deal of time idling. This means extra fuel burned and money wasted on something that isn't getting your business anywhere. In order to save money on fuel, it is important to have an understanding of how much fuel your truck uses per mile and what factors affect the amount of fuel used per mile.

There are two basic types of trucks: diesel and gasoline powered trucks. Diesel engines are more efficient than gasoline engines and they also use less energy than gasoline engines for every mile driven (11% less). This means that diesel engines use less fuel for every mile driven than their gasoline counterparts. However, this does not mean that you should always go with a diesel engine if you have the choice between a gasoline or diesel-powered truck as the cost difference between these two types of engines can be quite dramatic (as much as 1/3 cheaper).

The type of transmission in your truck will affect how much fuel you use as well: manual transmissions are more efficient than automatic transmissions. This is because manual transmissions use less energy to accelerate and they also have better fuel economy on the highway than automatic transmissions do.

There are a number of other factors that can affect your truck's fuel economy as well: weight, aerodynamics, and engine technology all play a role in determining how much fuel your truck uses per mile.

One of the best ways to decrease fuel costs is to take advantage of fuel efficiency technologies. Some of the best ways to do this include:

Keep your truck in good working order.

Maintain your truck's tires properly (tire pressure, tread, and wheel alignment).

Use less weight in your trailer. If you have a heavy load it will use more energy to move than a lighter load would. This is because there is more energy required to move large loads than small loads. So, fill your trailer up with as much product as you can without overloading it (something that can add substantial weight). Keep the weight in your trailer low by using lighter packaging materials and keeping boxes as empty as you can get them (leave room for cushioning material). Using heavier packaging materials will cost you extra money just for this reason. If you have air bags in your trailer consider removing them especially if they are rated at 1/2 ton or less as they are likely not worth their weight and space they take up, particularly if they are leaking or damaged (which is common). Another way to reduce the weight in your trailer is by using alternative packaging materials like plastic pallets instead of wood pallets or even bags instead of pallets if possible. Another alternative is to have your product shipped in bulk, but this can end up costing you more than you planned.

Replace your engine with a more fuel-efficient engine if possible as this will reduce the amount of fuel your truck uses per mile significantly. If you need to stay with your current engine, consider upgrading to the most efficient engine available for your model truck. Most trucks come with a "High Efficiency" or "Supercharged" engine option (if they are available for your model truck) that will save you money on fuel.

Use an aerodynamic trailer if possible as this will help keep drag down and decrease the amount of energy required to move it down the road. If you don't have an aerodynamic trailer, then consider pulling a trailer cover behind it to help keep drag down and save some gas. This is particularly useful if you are hauling heavy loads or driving long distances at highway speeds. Be sure that the trailer cover has vents built into it so that air can flow through and do not cover up all of the truck's lights as this will make it hard for other drivers to see you at night (which is extremely dangerous). Also be sure not to drive too fast when using a trailer cover as doing so will not only increase your fuel consumption but it will also impair your vision. It is advisable to keep your speed under 65 mph when using a trailer cover.

Consider a manual transmission if you have the choice between a manual or automatic transmission as they are more fuel efficient than automatic transmissions. Consider replacing an automatic transmission with a manual transmission if possible. If you don't have the option of either then drive slower and keep your speed under 65 mph on the highway as this will improve your fuel economy dramatically.

Keep an eye on how much fuel you use per mile and try not to exceed that amount so that you can keep your costs down. If you are using more than that amount, consider making some changes to reduce your fuel consumption (or simply spending less money on other things).

Hiring Employees

When you begin to hire employees, you will need to decide how much training and supervision you will have for them. Will you train them yourself or get other employees to train them? How much in-house training will you provide? You may have to be willing to pay more for employees with the right qualifications. Also, it may be important to have someone on the road with your drivers so that they can build a relationship with each other.

It is also possible that you can hire drivers who already know how to drive trucks, but they are underpaid and undertrained by their current employers. You can take these drivers and train them yourself, or you can use your own already trained employees (if any) to train them. In either case, it is a good idea to check references before making offers of employment.

You should also consider how much time it takes for a new employee to reach full productivity at your company. This is especially important if your business is seasonal, as it may take extra time for a new employee to be productive during a slow period.

How to Hire the Best Driver

This is a very important and difficult decision, so you should take the time to do it right. It is possible to hire drivers without ever meeting them, but this can be dangerous. If you do not know your drivers very well, then you cannot be sure that they are doing the job properly. Also, if you have no personal relationship with your drivers then they will not feel obligated to stay at your company for any extended period of time. You must be able to trust them greatly in order for them to work for you effectively and in order for them to stay with your company long-term.

When hiring a driver, one of the first things you should look at is their driving record. You want to see that their driving record does not involve any major accidents or tickets (especially moving violations). You also want to see that they have been working as a truck driver for at least two years (preferably more). The longer they have been driving trucks, the more drivers they will know and the more professional references they will have. This will help you avoid hiring a "rookie" driver who may not know how to drive safely on the road or who may be unreliable.

You should also check with their previous employers, and you may want to conduct a reference check. This will give you an idea of how your potential drivers will interact with others and how they handle stress. You also want to check their driving records to see if they have any violations for driving under the influence or for any "aggressive" driving incidents. If they have any of these problems in their history, then you probably should not hire them. You want drivers who are driven by safety, not by a desire to make as many miles as possible without food breaks or sleep.

You should also look at the company that the driver is currently working for or was working for previously. If they were fired from previous companies, then this is not a good sign. If they left on their own accord, then this could be a good thing—but you should still make sure that the reason why they left is valid (i.e., it was not due to laziness or another negative attribute). Don't be afraid to ask them about their previous job history—if there's something negative in their past, then it's better that you know about it up-front so that you can avoid hiring them and having problems later on.

Once you have narrowed down your choices and found the most qualified candidates, you can take the next step of choosing the best one. You should consider your own personal preferences when making this decision. If you prefer a conservative driver who follows all of the traffic laws, then you should choose that person over a more aggressive driver who may be a better choice for your company in other ways. The key is to make sure that the person you choose will fit into your company and will drive safely on the road.

How to Negotiate a Driver Contract

This is one of the most important contracts you will have to sign. It is also one of the most important decisions you will make for your company, so be sure to take your time and do it right.

A driver contract should cover a number of areas, including:

- The pay scale (i.e., what each mile's pay is)
- The amount of money the driver will receive when they are behind the wheel and when they are not driving (for example, waiting for loads or at lunch)
- How many hours per day that they will drive (for example, 11-13 hours per day), and how many days in a row that they can drive without taking a break (for example, 7 days)
- How much training the driver will get from you or another employee before going out on their own (if any)
- Any benefits that the driver will receive from you while working for your company (e.g., uniforms, fuel discounts, etc.)

The first thing to do is to decide how much you are willing to pay for each mile that your drivers drive. You should also consider how much you will pay when they are not driving, as this can be a significant part of your expenses. You may also consider using bonuses and incentives for your drivers. This will help you attract the best drivers and reward them for good performance.

Next, decide how many hours per day your drivers can drive. That is to say, how many hours per day will they be on the road? Also, how many consecutive days can they work without taking a break (e.g., 7 days)? For example, if you set their schedule at 11–12 hours per day with an 8-day maximum driving period, then your driver would be sitting in the truck for 2–3 days waiting for a load. This could be used for training or it could be used to make money by picking up extra loads during these periods of time—it's up to you and what you negotiate with your driver.

Also, don't forget to include any other costs in the contract that may come up regularly (i.e., uniforms or fuel discounts). Finally, if there are any benefits that the driver will receive, then you should include those in the contract as well (e.g., health insurance, retirement plan, etc.).

You should also consider a probationary period for your driver. This is a period of time where both you and the driver can evaluate each other and decide if this is a good fit for both of you. It's usually best to have this period last at least 30–45 days and it should be written into your contract as such. This will help both of you feel comfortable with the arrangement and it will prevent either party from feeling like they are trapped in a bad situation.

Finally, make sure that all of the terms are clearly defined in the contract so that there is no confusion about what each party must do or about what benefits they will receive during their employment with your company. A poorly drafted driver contract can lead to problems for both you and your drivers— it's best to have everything clearly defined up-front so that there will be no surprises later on.

Here is a sample contract for your drivers to sign:

Trucking Contract for Owner-Operator Truck Driver

_____

_____

Notice: This is a binding contract. If the driver does not fulfill all requirements, then he or she must pay damages in the amount of $5,000 per violation.

This contract is made by and between _____, who will be known as the "Truck Driver" and _____, who will be known as the "Company." The effective date of this contract is _____/_____/_____.

The Truck Driver agrees to drive for Company in trucks owned or leased by Company (Vehicles), during which time he/she will drive according to Company's rules and regulations. The Truck Driver agrees that he/she will not allow any other person to drive the Vehicles unless approved by the Company. The Truck Driver agrees that he/she will keep all log books in proper order according to state and federal laws. The Truck Driver agrees that he/she will not allow any child or other person under 18 years of age to be in the Vehicles when they are moving. The Truck Driver agrees that he/she will not use the Devices, including cellular telephones and PDAs, for any purpose other than business calls or messages while driving unless such use is approved by the Company. The Truck

Driver agrees to follow all applicable trucking laws and regulations.

The Company agrees to pay the Truck Driver at least $_____ for each hour that the Truck Driver is on duty and $_____ per mile driven in accordance with the rules and regulations of the Company. In addition, the Company agrees to provide a fuel card to be used by the Truck Driver for purchasing gasoline/diesel for Vehicles. The fuel card will be started at $_____ after which it may not exceed $_____ per month without prior approval from the Company. The Company also agrees to pay expenses incurred by the Truck Driver while traveling on Company business, including expenses for meals, lodging, and parking. These expenses will be calculated at _____ cents per mile each way (round trip) plus an additional _____ cents per mile if overnight lodging is required while traveling on business (this includes hotels, motels, or similar overnight accommodations). The Company also agrees to pay for all repairs and maintenance of the Vehicles.

The Company will deduct the following from the paychecks of the Truck Driver:

Social Security Taxes (6%) _____ Medicare Taxes (1.45%) _____ Federal Income Tax (from wages only) _____ State Income Tax (from wages only) _____ Unemployment Insurance Taxes (from wages only) _____ Worker's Compensation Insurance Premiums (from wages only) _____ Other Deductions as Required by Law or Company Policy _____ Total Amount Deductions _____ Net Pay Amount $_____, which is to be paid on a weekly basis or twice monthly at Company's discretion.

The Company agrees to provide the Truck Driver with reasonable amounts of fuel and oil when necessary to run the Vehicles. The amount of fuel provided will be determined by necessity according to state and federal laws. The amount of fuel purchased by a Truck Driver on his/her own time will not exceed $_____ per week without prior approval from the Company. If a driver needs additional fuel beyond what is provided by Company while he/she is operating vehicles for other companies, then he/she must use his/her own money or obtain approval from Company prior to using his/her fuel card.

The Company agrees to provide the Truck Driver with a phone, a radio, and cellular telephone service for use in the Vehicles. The number of calls made on cellular telephones will not exceed $_____ per week without prior approval from the Company. All calls made on cellular telephones for personal use will be deducted from that amount, and all calls made on Company-provided phones for personal use must be reimbursed by the Truck Driver at least $_____ per minute. In addition, the Company agrees to pay for any lost or stolen equipment that is replaced by the Truck Driver. The total company-provided equipment that may be used in the Vehicles is _____.

If any of these rules or regulations are violated by the Truck Driver, then he/she must pay the Company $5,000 to cover any damages or losses incurred by the Company as a result of such violation. This payment must be made within _____ days after such violation occurs, and it must be paid before returning to work for the Company again. If these rules or regulations are violated by anyone other than the Truck Driver, then he/she must immediately dismiss such person from employment with no further compensation due.

The Company agrees to provide $_____ for each day that the Truck Driver works for the Company. This money will be paid at the end of each week or twice monthly at the discretion of the Company.

All other rules and regulations are as follows:

_____
_____
_____
_____
_____
_____
_____

This Contract is to be signed by: _____, the "Company" and _____, the "Truck Driver." Both parties agree to abide by all of the rules in this contract. If either party does not keep all of these rules, then he/she must pay a penalty of $5,000. This is a binding contract between both parties. This contract is effective on _____ and ends on _____.

Work Schedule Planning

One of the most important things to consider is your work schedule. When most people think of the trucking industry, they think of truckers on the road on a long haul, driving overnight. This is only one part of the picture. You can operate your business in several different ways:

Long Haul Trucking

This type of work schedule is what most people think about when they think about the trucking business. The driver works for a company and drives a long distance. He or she will have time at home, possibly be home every other weekend, and then head out again. The company will generally pay for some type of housing when the driver is away from home, and then pay for hotels when it makes sense to stop for fuel or other needs. This type of schedule involves trucks that are up to 20 feet in length with 48-foot - 53-foot trailers. While this method makes sense for some drivers who are single or married with no children, it does not make sense for others who want to have more time at home with their families.

Local Trucking

Local trucking is something that has become popular in recent years. This type of trucking involves driving a truck that is up to 20 feet long and a trailer that is 28 - 36 feet long. There are numerous companies that use this type of setup. The benefit to this type of work schedule is that the drivers will be home every day. They will typically have a regular shift, such as 6am to 4pm or 7am to 3pm. Some companies will allow you to start earlier and work later in exchange for more time off at other times of the year.

Hybrid Trucking

Hybrid trucking is the combination of long haul and local trucking schedules. You may drive the long haul, but then you may spend some time in your home city as well as drive shorter distances while on the road. This type of schedule often makes sense for certain drivers who want a variety of driving while still being able to come home most nights.

Make sure that you do not plan your work schedule based on what you think is best for you. You need to take into consideration the needs of your family and of yourself. In addition, you need to consider whether or not this type of schedule will be sustainable in the long run. Some drivers are able to work on this type of schedule without too much trouble, but others find that it does not make sense due to a lack of down time between shifts or being too tired at home because they are driving all day and then having to do things when they get home.

Truck Scheduling Software

There are numerous types of software that can help you with your truck scheduling. Be sure to take the time to find out about the options that are available to you and then figure out which program will work best for you. You may be able to find a program that is free or low cost, but it is important to look at the features available in comparison to what you are willing to spend. In addition, there are programs that might be more expensive, but will include additional features that make it worth your time and money.

Most programs will allow you to schedule your work based on a variety of factors. They will allow you to enter all of your commitments and then use a calendar or other tool within the program itself in order to create a schedule that meets all of your needs. You may have daily activities such as spending time with your family or taking care of household chores, and then you may have long-term commitments such as holidays or vacation plans for your family. Your schedule needs to take all of these into account if it is going to work well for everyone involved.

Some companies have tried entering their work schedules manually into a spreadsheet type format and then having drivers log their actual hours into the spreadsheet as time goes on throughout the week or month. While this can work for one driver, it does not work well for any drivers that are working in different locations or on a different schedule. This method also leads to some issues when drivers have to take longer than expected breaks or if they end up working late.

The easiest way to create a schedule is to use software that allows you to input all of your commitments into the program and then set up a time frame that matches your needs. You may be able to plan your work based on weekly, biweekly, or monthly commitments. You can also plan based on individual days if you need more flexibility in your schedule. Once you have created the schedule, you can then use the program itself in order to see when each individual driver needs to be where in order to meet all of these commitments.

It is important that you view the schedule several times over the course of a few days so that you can make sure that it works as well as possible before handing it off to your employees for their use. It is possible that there are some issues with the schedule, such as someone who does not have enough time between shifts. When you are creating a schedule, you need to take into consideration all of the factors that will impact it. You need to look for issues that might cause problems for drivers and others who work in your company.

When scheduling your drivers, you should consider the following:

How far do they live from the facility? Why is this important? If some of your drivers live extremely far away, then it might make sense to allow them to start early in order to give them more time for driving home instead of working later. If they can get home earlier but they are still going to have a long day, then this is something that you will want to take into consideration when creating their work schedule.

What does the driver do during his or her down time? Why is this important? Some drivers enjoy relaxing when they are not driving a truck. They may enjoy taking time off after a long day or even spending part of their days doing household chores like mowing the lawn or walking the dog instead of resting up before heading back out on the road again. Other drivers may not be able to relax very easily and may prefer setting up an activity during their free time such as watching TV or running errands instead of sitting around at home doing nothing. It is important that you consider the needs of each of your drivers. You do not want to create a schedule that makes it difficult for one driver to be able to relax while at home.

What is the driving experience of the driver? Why is this important? If your drivers are used to driving short distances, then it might make sense to allow them to drive locally instead of long distance. They may work better on shorter shifts and they may be more comfortable with driving smaller trucks. On the other hand, if they have experience driving long distances, then it might make sense for them to continue driving long distances. They will be more comfortable on longer shifts and it is likely that they will have more experience in this type of environment as well.

What type of trucking company is your business? Why is this important? Some companies operate as owner-operators and some are strictly fleet operators. An owner-operator trucking company will typically allow their drivers more flexibility in their schedules than a fleet operator does, but a fleet operator will provide additional support in other areas such as maintenance and safety training which an owner-operator will need to pay for out of pocket. While both types of companies can work well in many situations, you need to think about your business and the type of schedules that you will need to run in order to ensure that you are operating in the best way possible.

What type of trucking business do you run? Why is this important? Some companies have a mix of long distance and local driving, while some companies will specialize in one or the other. This is an important consideration when creating your work schedule as well. If your drivers are used to driving long distances, then it might make sense to have them drive long distances all of the time instead of mixing it with local driving. If they are used to local driving, then it might make sense for them to do more local driving than long distance.

What types of trucks do you own? Why is this important? Some drivers prefer one type of truck over another. They may feel more comfortable in a small truck that has limited space than they do in a larger truck with more space. You need to take into consideration the needs of each driver as well as their preferences. If you have a driver who does not like driving a certain type of truck, then it might make sense for him or her not to drive that type of truck during certain times or at certain places if possible.

The best operating strategies are the ones that you create based on your own unique situation and the needs of your drivers. You need to consider a number of factors in order to determine how things will operate for each individual driver. There is no one size fits all solution when it comes to scheduling drivers.

Equipment Maintenance and Repair

Trucking is a harsh environment for vehicles. With the miles that they travel, the wear and tear that they endure, and the elements that they deal with on a daily basis, trucks are exposed to difficult conditions. The maintenance and repair of these vehicles is one of the major expenses for an owner-operator.

Maintenance

The vehicle maintenance can be divided into two categories: routine maintenance and repair. Routine maintenance includes oil changes, tire rotations, fluid flushes, and minor engine repairs. It is recommended to have routine maintenance performed by a service professional at least once every 100,000 miles or every year. When it comes to tires, you should replace them when they have approximately 5/32nds of tread remaining on their surfaces. If you are running on bald tires, you will not be able to drive at high speeds or make sharp turns because the tread will be worn down too much. This can lead to accidents or flats that can cost thousands of dollars in repairs. Fluid checks/flushes should be done approximately every 10,000–15,000 miles (depending on your vehicle) in order to maintain your engine's efficiency; this includes transmission fluid changes (if applicable), coolant flushes (if applicable), brake fluid changes, and power steering fluid changes.

Repairs

Repairing damages to a vehicle is more expensive than maintaining it. This is because repairs are done in order to continue operating the vehicle, while routine maintenance is done to ensure the efficiency of the vehicle. Repairs are also less predictable than routine maintenance. The cost of repairs varies based on the amount of damage that was sustained during an accident or the wear and tear that was done by normal use. The owner-operator should try to fix damages as soon as possible, if they can afford it, so that they can continue driving immediately without having to wait for parts or pay someone else to do it for them. If you are not able to repair the damages yourself, either due to lack of time or lack of tools/vehicle knowledge, you should try to find someone who can do it for free, such as family members or friends. If this is not possible then you should go ahead and pay someone else for their services (preferably a mechanic since they have experience). The only time when paying someone else for repairs is recommended is when you need an immediate fix before you head out on a long-haul trip; in this case taking your truck off the road for a week or more will be more expensive than paying someone else to fix it.

Truck maintenance is very important because it ensures that your truck is in good working order at all times. If your truck is properly maintained, you will not have to worry about unexpected problems occurring while you are on the road. If a problem does occur, however, you should try to fix it as soon as possible, especially if it occurs during a long-haul trip or when a load needs to be delivered on time. If you are unable to solve the problem yourself, ask someone who knows how to fix vehicles for help; try family members and friends first before asking strangers for help. The last resort would be taking your truck off the road for repairs; this could cost thousands of dollars in lost revenue but is necessary when the safety of the vehicle is in question. When it comes to maintenance and repairs of your truck, remember that it is better to spend money now in order to avoid spending money later on an emergency repair or an accident caused by damaged parts.

The most common repairs that you will need to make to your vehicle due to damage or normal wear and tear are:

Tire Replacement

The most common damage that a truck will sustain is a flat tire. It is recommended to replace tires every five years, but if you drive in bad weather (snow, rain, etc.) or over rough roads (such as rocky or dirt roads) then it is best to replace them more frequently.

Windshield Repair

If you have sustained damages from rocks or other debris, your windshield may crack from the impact. If this happens, you should have it repaired by a professional as soon as possible so that your vision isn't impaired while driving next time; however, if the crack is not too large, you can install an aftermarket windshield on your own for less than $100 before getting it repaired professionally at $200 and up.

Oil Change

When you change the oil on your vehicle, it is recommended that you change the oil filter as well since it is pretty inexpensive and usually not too difficult to do.

Tire Rotation

Rotation of tires is recommended every 5,000–10,000 miles to ensure even wear and tear of tires. This process can be done yourself or by a service professional for a small fee.

Engine Repair

If you have an engine problem, have it fixed as soon as possible so that it doesn't damage anything else under the hood. If you are not sure about how to repair the engine yourself, find a mechanic who can fix it for you and pay them for their services.

Brake Pad Replacement

Your truck will need new brake pads when they are worn down past certain levels; if this happens, you should replace them immediately because brakes are critical to stopping your vehicle when it is moving at high speeds. The best time to do this is at the beginning of long-haul trips so that your brakes don't get damaged on the way there or back. It will cost around $100 to replace them yourself if they are simple enough, but if they need special tools or parts then it can cost up to $400 to replace them.

Power Steering Fluid Replacement

If your power steering fluid is leaking out of your vehicle, have it replaced as soon as possible so that it doesn't cause any further damage to the power steering pump or belt. You can either buy the fluid yourself and replace it with the help of a service manual, or you can pay someone to do it for you. It will cost around $200 to replace it with the help of a service manual, and $400 if you pay someone else to do it.

Air Filter Replacement

You should change your air filter before each long-haul trip if possible, just because they get dirty after driving for long periods of time and will make your truck run less efficiently than normal; however, if you are not taking any trips soon, you can wait until your next oil change and have them change it at the same time. The air filter itself costs around $20–$30 and a professional mechanic will charge about $100 for their services; so, if you have time before your next trip then replacing your air filter will be cheaper than paying a mechanic to do it for you.

Exhaust Repair

If there is excessive damage to your exhaust system then this will need to be repaired as soon as possible so that you can continue to drive your truck without any further damage. If the damage is not too extensive, you can repair it yourself with the help of a service manual, but if it is more extensive then you should have a professional mechanic fix it for you; it will cost around $200 to repair it yourself, and $800–$1000 if you pay someone else.

Engine Replacement

If your engine is damaged beyond repair then the owner-operator will need to replace it with a new one; this will cost between $2,500–$4,000 depending on the make and model of your truck.

Brake Job

The brakes on your truck are critical to keeping you safe while driving and if they are not working properly then they need to be repaired as soon as possible; when dealing with brakes there is no such thing as too much maintenance. When dealing with brake jobs, the owner-operator should make sure they have all of the tools needed for any repairs before attempting them because if they break something that was not broken before (e.g. brake lines) then they will have to pay double for their services since they broke something while repairing something else. It is recommended that an owner-operator takes their vehicle into a mechanic to have them do the repairs, but if time is a factor then they can try to fix it themselves with the help of a service manual; if this is the case then they should do some research on how to repair their specific vehicle before attempting to do so. It will cost between $300 and $1,000 depending on your vehicle and what exactly needs to be repaired.

Engine Oil/Filter Replacement

If you have not replaced your engine oil or filter in a long time then consider doing so because it is fairly inexpensive (around $50) and it will ensure that your engine runs at maximum efficiency.

Tire Plug

If you are driving on a highway and one of your tires becomes damaged past the point where you can drive on it safely, then you can plug it by using a tire plug kit. This will allow you to drive safely until you reach your destination where you can replace the tire properly. The cost of these kits will vary based on where they are purchased from, but they generally cost around $20–$30 per kit.

Chapter 5: Growth Strategies

Just about every entrepreneur dreams of the day when they can build a successful business and, in the process, become financially independent. For the small business owner, perhaps the most attractive reason for achieving this goal is the freedom it brings, the freedom to take a vacation when you want to, or do something that interests you on a whim. For trucking business owners, this freedom is manifested in many ways, which include flexibility in where you live and a lifestyle free from the restrictions of working for someone else.

The challenges of starting a business are many, but the rewards are even greater. To illustrate this point, when you build a business, you are building a house from scratch. Just as building a house requires concrete blocks for the foundation and shingles to cover it, starting your own business also requires certain things that must be in place before you can begin to build it—things like transportation and financing. Just like houses need floors and walls, businesses need products or services that can be sold. The goal is to provide the highest level of quality for your customers so they will continue to buy from you in the future. The more clients you have now, the easier it will be to acquire new ones later down the road when your customer base is larger. Your main focus at this point must be on gaining new customers, but if possible, also retain existing customers as well. One way of doing this is by offering them incentives for being repeat customers such as coupons or discounts on their next purchase or service.

Whether you decide to start out as an owner-operator or hire a driver to do it for you, the business plan is still the same. The difference is that you will be handling all the day-to-day operations yourself, and if you hire someone else to drive for you, then it's your responsibility to recruit and hire drivers.

Let's take a look at what it takes to scale your business.

Advertising for Freight

There are many ways to advertise for freight, but one of the most effective ways is by using a broker. Brokers are companies that provide transportation services by matching trucking companies with shippers looking for transportation services. They are commonly referred to as "shipper's brokers" or "carrier's brokers." These companies can be found locally and on the Internet and work on commission. The advantage of working with a broker is that they have access to more freight than you possibly could have in your area, and they will provide you with all of the information you need about each load and where it needs to be delivered.

For owner-operators, there are also a number of websites that allow you to advertise your load requirements, so for those who want to take that approach it might be worth looking into as well. Some of the most popular ones are: www.hotshottrucking.com and www.thebrokerlist.com.

In addition, you can also advertise in trucking magazines for loads. You can find these magazines at truck stops, rest areas, and convenience stores near the interstate.

You can also advertise for loads on the radio, which is comparatively cheaper than other forms of advertising such as TV ads.

Regardless of how you choose to advertise for freight, there are three things to remember:

1. Provide your information as completely as possible for maximum exposure.
2. Be the first to respond to the load.
3. Remain professional at all times and be prepared for any situation that arises.

If you're not able to get enough business through advertising, then you can always go back to your broker or freight-matching website and ask for a load, but if you decide to do this then make sure you know the rate that's going to be paid so you don't waste your time with loads that won't pay enough money.

Marketing Strategies That Work

Whether you are an owner-operator or a small business, marketing is one of the most important aspects of running a trucking business. You must market your business to potential customers and existing clients in order to keep up with expenses and stay competitive.

In today's competitive marketplace, marketing strategies that work will help you to gain more clients, retain existing clients, and improve your image in the eyes of the public as a reliable and professional company. In addition, there are many ways to market your trucking company for free through Internet marketing methods. One popular method is by creating a website that portrays your individual style as well as the services you offer. This site should be professionally designed so it is easy for visitors to use and understand and should be updated frequently with current information about your business. Another way is through blogging on social media sites such as Facebook and Twitter which can be very effective if done properly.

Of course, another cost-effective way to advertise is through radio advertising. You can either hire an advertising agency or do it yourself depending on how much money you have to spend on advertising. However, if you decide to do it yourself then make sure you know what information needs to be included in each ad so they are effective.

You should also consider attending different local events and making it a habit to talk with people. In this way, you will get to know your potential clients and build relationships with them, but remember that the key here is to constantly promote your business and not just attend one event and then disappear.

If you already have clients then consider using print advertising such as newspaper ads or magazines they may read. This approach can be very effective if done correctly and professionally written. When writing your ad, remember that it's better to write fewer words that will catch the reader's attention than to write more words that will cause him or her to gloss over it altogether. If you want someone to take action from reading your ad then you must provide enough information so they know exactly what they are getting into when they work with you but not so much information that you lose their attention completely.

One of the most common mistakes that trucking companies make when marketing their business is offering discounts for new clients or first-time business owners. Because of this, many companies just end up losing money on each load because the freight rates are not high enough in order for them to make any profits on each load or individual transaction. If you decide to give discounts, then make sure they are small and you are able to offer them for a limited time period.

If you want to be more successful in your trucking business, then consider marketing yourself as a leader in the industry—someone who can provide quality service to your clients. In order for you to do this successfully you must first learn how to provide high-quality service by reading up on industry trends and listening to your clients. Also consider learning how to market your company so that it has a respectable image in the eyes of the public, because when customers see ads for your company it will increase their trust in what they are reading.

Negotiating Freight Rates

The rate that you're going to get paid is going to depend on the type of load you're transporting and the length of time it takes to complete. The rate is usually determined by taking into account the distance traveled, the weight of the load, and how quickly it must be delivered. To determine what rate you'll be paid by a shipper for a particular load, take the weight of the load, multiply it by the price per pound for that type of freight, and then add in any other charges such as fuel surcharges or tolls along with any other fees that may be involved. Then divide this number by your daily mileage. If you're working out of state, divide your mileage by your miles per gallon so you can calculate how many gallons are used per mile. Then multiply that number by the price per gallon for diesel fuel in your area. This will give you an approximate amount of what it will cost to operate your truck for a day. Some carriers also factor in their labor expenses when calculating their rates, but this isn't always necessary since their labor expenses usually have little impact on their overall profit margin as they are already included in their overall operational costs.

To negotiate the best rate possible, you need to prepare for the negotiation by identifying which loads you'd like to take along with the ones that you already have. After that, contact your broker and ask them to get you a rate for the load that you want. If they can't get it then go ahead and get a rate for the load that you have. When negotiating with the shipper, be sure to ask how long it will take to complete the load; it doesn't do any good to negotiate a higher rate if it takes you too long to deliver it. You should also ask what type of freight it is, how heavy it is, where will they be shipping from, and where will they be shipping to. This information will help determine how much time is needed for delivery as well as what fuel surcharges or tolls might be involved in getting there.

After this information has been gathered, begin negotiating your daily rate. You should first try negotiating a flat per mile rate instead of having them charge by the hour as this will give you more flexibility in your route planning and allow you to come up with more optimal routes. Negotiating your rates on a per mile basis can also help reduce your operating expenses, and if you're also negotiating your fuel surcharges then this will help you save even more money. The rate that they initially give you is going to be below market value, so don't feel bad when you counteroffer a higher rate. You might have to try several different rates before they are willing to go with your most recent offer. In most cases, the shipper wants to pay as little as possible since it's their cost that they are trying to keep down. You also need to be aware of the fact that you may be the only carrier in the area that's available for this load so they may be forced to take what they can get and settle for a rate closer to your initial offer. If this is the case then consider yourself lucky because it means that you have a captive audience and can negotiate a better rate later on when another carrier becomes available.

When negotiating with a shipper, never accept their offer right away but always counter offer an amount higher than what they gave you. If you do this, they will usually gladly accept your most recent counteroffer and tell you that it sounds like an agreement has been reached and begin preparing their paperwork for delivery of the load. However, be careful when doing this since they may be just trying to trick you into accepting their first offer.

The key to negotiating is being prepared. Know the type of load you're transporting, how long it will take to complete, the type of freight it is, where it's going to be shipped from, and where it's going to be shipped to. Also know how much time is needed for delivery as well as what fuel surcharges or tolls might be involved in getting there.

Be Part of Truck Associations

There are a number of trucking associations out there that you can join. Not only can these associations be a great source of information and networking opportunities, but they also offer many benefits that could help your business. Some of the most popular trucking associations include:

- Owner-Operator Independent Drivers Association (OOIDA)
- American Trucking Associations (ATA)
- American Trucking Associations of Canada (ATAC)
- Canadian Trucking Alliance (CTA)
- Coalition for Transportation Productivity (CTP)

These organizations typically offer discounts on roadside service, health insurance, and other benefits that you might find useful in running your business. They also provide information about safety practices as well as industry news that you would otherwise not be aware of. They provide services such as roadside assistance 24 hours a day, 365 days a year, and an around-the-clock toll-free hotline if you have any questions or concerns regarding your trucking business. In addition, many of these associations offer seminars designed to help their members run a successful business.

Another important benefit of joining trucking associations is the opportunity to network and meet other drivers. When you meet other drivers, you will learn about their business model as well as how they go about handling certain issues specific to the trucking business. There are also opportunities to join trucking forums and blogs where you can ask questions and get answers from industry experts.

What are the fees involved?

Joining a trucking association is not mandatory, but it's highly recommended. The amount of fees you will be required to pay will depend on the association you choose and the type of membership you select. For example, if you are an owner-operator wanting to join a trucking association, then you may have to pay more than an individual who wants to join as a driver. Some associations may also charge a one-time joining fee and an annual membership fee as well. Fees are usually nominal but can range anywhere from $35-$300 per year.

What kind of benefits should I expect?

The benefits that these associations offer will vary depending on the specific organization that you join as well as what type of membership you select. The most common benefits include:

- Discounts on health insurance plans and roadside assistance service for your truck
- Seminars and workshops designed to help members run their business more profitably and efficiently
- Access to industry news, updates, blogs, and forums where members can ask questions or share information with other individuals in the industry

Some associations even offer member discounts when doing business with companies such as auto dealerships which offer items such as truck parts, tires, and other accessories.

Finding Funding

One of the biggest challenges you will face is finding funding. Even if you pay everything out of your own pocket, which is always a good idea until you have a steady source of income, there will still be some expenses that are unavoidable. These include things like the initial purchase price of the truck and insurance, licensing fees and permits, plus fuel for running it, and an office to operate it from. If you decide to start out as an owner-operator, then what you need is a home base. The best thing about this approach is that you don't have to worry about finding drivers—you do it yourself.

If you decide to hire drivers, then having a home base is still important because you need somewhere safe for them to park while they are not on the road delivering goods. Of course, they can also stay there while they are off duty if they choose. You can also keep their personal belongings in a lock box in your office or in their truck so nothing gets stolen when they aren't around. You may even want to offer them some perks such as discounted meals at fast food restaurants or free laundry services so they don't have to spend extra time looking for places to eat or wash their clothes.

Here are some ways that you can find investors for your business.

Friends and Family

Although this source of funding may be the most obvious, it is also the least reliable. Although you may expect your family members and friends to be willing to help you out, there is always a chance that they will back out of the deal or change their minds about it after they have put in some money. This can happen even if they have promised you that they will do so, so don't take anything for granted.

Banks

The next place to look is a bank or credit union. You will probably need some collateral for a loan from them, but if you are starting out as an owner-operator then there should be no problem with this since you will be using the truck as collateral. If you decide to hire drivers then the value of the fleet will increase with each new driver that joins and your credit rating will improve as well, which should make things easier when it comes time to apply for a loan or line of credit from a bank or other financial institution.

Venture Capitalists

If you want to start a business that does not require a large initial investment then this is the way to go. All you will need are some good ideas and a willingness to work hard to see them through. You may even be able to find investors who will give you money for free if they think your idea has enough potential.

Use Your Assets

If you already have some assets, such as real estate or stocks and bonds, then it may be possible for you to use these as collateral for a loan. However, the interest rate on these types of loans is usually higher than what is available from banks and credit unions, so consider all your options before taking out such a loan.

Use Your Own Capital

This is always an option if you have some money saved up or can borrow money from somewhere else without charging interest on it. Just remember that there will be no returns on this investment unless it turns out to be successful.

Using your own capital makes sense if this venture will help grow other areas of your business or even help fund other future ventures. Just make sure that you take into account the expense of equipment and other operating costs when deciding whether or not this is the right thing to do.

Loans and Lines of Credit

Scaling your business usually means increasing the number of customers that you serve. As the business grows, it will need more cash to support the increase in business, but when you start out you don't have that much to invest and what you do have may be tied up in the truck. You can get a loan for your truck from a bank or a financial institution such as an SBA (Small Business Administration) office, but these loans are tough to get without any collateral. This is why most owner-operators initially finance their trucks with a personal loan from their local credit union or bank. It's easier to get approved for this type of loan because banks and credit unions believe that if you buy a truck using your own money then you probably have enough income coming in from other sources to pay them back as well.

There are two ways of getting financing when starting out: taking out a personal loan or borrowing against your home equity.

Home Equity

If you decide to borrow against your home equity, this would require selling another type of insurance called an "equity life insurance policy" which would pay off the debt and keep your home in case anything happens to you before you can pay off the debt yourself. Another potential problem is that if you go this route, then the bank or credit union will probably require a co-signer on your loan, someone who has good credit and financial standing.

Personal Loan

If you can't get a co-signer then you have to be extra careful about the kind of personal loan you take out. Banks and credit unions are usually more lenient with personal loans than they are with business loans because they assume that personal loans are for items like your car, vacations, or college education. On the other hand, business loans are expected to be used for day-to-day expenses such as trucks, fuel, insurance, etc.

Capital Lease

In addition to a business line of credit and personal loan options for financing your trucking business there is one more alternative: using a "capital lease" as opposed to an "operating lease" when purchasing the truck. This would involve getting the truck financed through an independent leasing company such as ARI (American Fleet Management) or US Lease Finance Corporation (USLFC). The difference between these two types of leases is that under an operating lease (or "rental agreement") you would be responsible for all maintenance and repairs yourself, while under a capital lease you can allow the leasing company to repair it for you, but at a cost. The advantage of using a capital lease is that you can deduct the monthly payments on the truck from your taxes as opposed to an operating lease where you are not allowed to deduct any of the payments, making your profits taxable.

Line of Credit

If you can afford to make larger payments on a personal loan, then a good way to save money is to apply for a "line of credit" at your local bank instead of a regular loan. The advantage of this is that you can put yourself on an automatic payment plan and save money by not having to pay any interest as long as you don't add any additional debt. The drawback is that if you run into trouble and have to take out an emergency loan, then you will probably have to pay the extra interest. If you use this type of line of credit, then it's important that you don't put yourself too close to your limit because if something goes wrong and you can't make the payments then they might end up repossessing the truck.

If you want to get approved for a business loan or line of credit from your bank or credit union without putting up collateral, then one way of doing this is by using your company name instead of your own name as a co-signer. For example, if you had a family member who could vouch for your business then they would be considered the co-signer. Or if there was another owner-operator who was willing to be your co-signer then you could go into your bank and ask for a business loan with his company name as the co-signer. However, this is a risky form of financing because if something happens to you then they could repossess the truck and sell it to pay off the debt.

Cash

If you are a new owner-operator who is struggling with getting approved for financing, then another option is to simply pay cash when buying the truck. There are many different ways of doing this: if you have a lot of money saved up, then you can simply save up and buy the truck outright using cash from your own bank account. You can also borrow money from friends or family members who trust that you will pay them back in a few months' time. Another way is to use one of your existing credit cards by paying it off immediately after getting approved for the loan or line of credit. Or if you don't have enough cash saved up, then another option is to use "factoring" which involves selling your accounts receivable (or invoices) to an independent factoring company such as Argon Factors which will advance part of the purchase price on your truck while waiting for your customers to pay their invoices.

Secured Credit Card

Another option is to use a "secured credit card" as opposed to a regular credit card. A secured credit card works just like a regular credit card, but instead of the bank or financial institution giving you money, you borrow against the money that you already have in your checking account. This would involve getting an unsecured credit card with high interest rates and then using it to buy whatever you need for your trucking business. You would pay off the balance every month with the money in your checking account, but if there was ever an emergency where you didn't have enough money in the checking account then they could take the truck. For example, if there was ever a situation where you needed extra cash and didn't want to just use another credit card then this could be a good alternative. The advantage is that they would only take one piece of property from you instead of all of them at once. The disadvantage is that if things don't work out and you can't make any more payments on it, then they will end up taking all of the property that they have a lien against (the truck) which could end up being a lot more than if you had just put it up as collateral for a business loan.

The other thing to consider is how long you will keep the truck before selling it. Even if you buy the truck outright or use a secured credit card, then there will still be expenses involved with buying and selling the truck such as registration fees, title transfer fees, etc. If you are going to take on outside financing then these costs can get added onto the loan or line of credit and paid off over time. If you decide to finance through an independent leasing company like ARI (American Rollover Inc.) then your only expenses would be monthly payments which could be higher than what the bank or credit union might charge you.

Another thing to consider is that almost all banks and credit unions require that you have two years' worth of business experience before they approve any type of loan or line of credit for your business.

When you first start out it's better not to take out any outside financing because if something goes wrong with your business then there will be more things for the bank or credit union to take away from you. However, if things are going well and your revenues are increasing at a steady rate, then this is a good time to start thinking about outside financing in order to expand your business.

Tax Deductibles

One of the ways that trucking companies can deduct some of their expenses is to claim the vehicle as a "second car" for the owner/operator. This gives him another deduction on his tax return.

The truck needs to be used for personal transportation, and you need a driver's license, but that's about it. If you want to use your truck as a second car, you can do so by following these steps:

Determine if You Will Use Your Truck as a Second Car

If your business is properly structured, and you have a good understanding of the IRS guidelines for deductibles, you may be able to write off your truck as a second car. It's important to know that the IRS is very strict about what is allowed for deduction, so be careful.

Determine if You Will Be Using Your Truck for Personal Use

If you plan on using your truck as a second car, it's important that it only be used for personal use. If you use the truck on company business, then you cannot claim it as a second car deduction.

Check with Your Insurance Company to see if You Can Claim a Second Car Deduction for Your Truck

Insurance companies vary widely in their willingness to allow truckers to claim their trucks as a second vehicle. Some will allow it with no problem at all, while others will not allow it under any circumstances. If your insurance company allows it, they will provide you with documentation proving the deduction, which will be required when filing your taxes.

Check with Your State to See if You Are Allowed to Claim a Second Car Deduction

Some states do not allow the deduction of a vehicle that is not completely used for business purposes. If you are unsure about whether or not your state allows this deduction, contact your state tax agency.

Determine if the Vehicle Will Be Used for Business Reasons and How Much of the Time It Will Be Used for Business Reasons

If you plan on using your vehicle as a second car, but also plan on using it for business reasons, you need to carefully document how much time it will be used for business versus personal use. If you are unsure about how to do this, consult with an accountant who specializes in trucking taxes and can help you figure out what is allowed and what is not allowed by the IRS.

Make Sure That You Can Prove All of These Things

Whether or not your vehicle can be claimed as a second car deduction depends entirely on whether or not you can prove that it was only used for personal reasons during the year. In order to prove this claim, you will need receipts and documentation from your insurance company showing proof that they allowed the claim.

Complete IRS Form 2106

In order to claim this deduction, you will need to complete the IRS form 2106, which is used for calculating your business deductions. This form is used in conjunction with Schedule A, which is used to itemize all of your deductible expenses. You will also need to fill out Schedule C of IRS Form 1040, and state tax forms as well. Your accountant can help you with this if you are unsure about how to complete these forms.

Include Your Deduction on Your Tax Return

And, finally, remember to include the deduction on your tax return and not your business return. This is a personal deduction and should be reported on your personal tax return.

The IRS has strict guidelines that must be followed in order to deduct a vehicle as a second car, and it's important to follow them exactly if you want to avoid an audit. If you want to make sure that you have done everything correctly, consult with an accountant who specializes in trucking taxes and can help you with the process.

Is fuel tax deductible?

The short answer is yes. The long answer is, it depends on the nature of your business and how you use the fuel.

If you are operating a sole proprietorship, you probably don't have a lot of tax deductions. However, if you are operating as a corporation, then that's a different story. If you operate as an LLC or partnership, then it's still possible to take a deduction for fuel expenses. You'll need to do some homework in order to make sure that your deduction is valid and that you can prove it with documentation. It's important to get it right because if you don't get it right, the IRS will disallow your deductions and could even send agents out to audit you. That would not be good considering the time involved in an audit.

But let's start with the basics first. If you operate as a sole proprietorship or LLC, there are still ways that you can deduct fuel costs by taking advantage of bonus depreciation on equipment purchases and/or capitalizing costs associated with equipment maintenance (cabin filters, oil changes, tune-ups). For example: if your corporation operates as an LLC or sole proprietorship (or another non-corporate entity), you can deduct the "depreciation" on a truck or a trailer.

How is depreciation calculated?

Depreciation is calculated based on the estimated useful life of your equipment. The IRS uses five-year increments. The first year has the highest depreciation and each year after that is less than the previous year. For example, in the first year, you could claim 100% of your equipment costs as a deduction. In the second year, you would be able to claim 95% of your equipment costs and so on for five years until you reach no deduction at all for any new purchases and only 50% of used equipment costs after that time period. This is called bonus depreciation and is special treatment from Congress to help business owners get their businesses off the ground or expand their operations.

It's also possible to take a deduction for fuel if you operate as a corporation with an LLC structure as well (or any other non-corporate entity). For example: if you have an LLC operating as a corporation (LLC), then it's possible to claim fuel deductions by treating them as capital expenses instead of operational expenses. This is often referred to by accountants who specialize in trucking taxes as "transportation" expenses versus "allowable" expenses. "Allowable" expenses are those that can be claimed for tax deductions by a corporation. For example, if you have an LLC that operates as a corporation, you can claim fuel costs as a capital expense and depreciate them over several years (according to the same schedule laid out above).

If you operate as an LLC or sole proprietorship (or any other non-corporate entity), claiming fuel costs as a capital expense is often referred to as "expensing." Although the IRS allows these types of businesses to take "allowable" expenses like fuel costs on their tax returns, they only allow a certain amount of these types of expenses before they disallow the rest. This is because the IRS does not want sole proprietors or LLCs to deduct all of their business expenses and pass the entire profit through to their personal returns. The IRS wants owners of non-corporate entities to pay at least some income taxes on their business profits. Therefore, it's important for businesses structured in this manner to carefully keep track of only those business expenses that are allowed for tax deduction and leave out personal operating costs like gas, oil changes, repairs, tolls, tires, and maintenance items like cabin filters and window scrapers.

As a business owner or an accountant who specializes in trucking taxes, you need to understand the difference between deductible expenses versus non-deductible expenses. This is very important. Otherwise, you could end up paying more in taxes than you are required to pay. For example: if you buy $5,000 worth of fuel for your business that year, but $2,500 of that fuel was used for personal purposes and not on business purposes, then the IRS will disallow your deduction on the entire $5,000 and tax you on the $2,500 that should not have been included in the first place. Therefore, it's important to keep track of all business and personal use of fuel and other expenses.

How is fuel used by a business allocated?

For tax purposes, it's important to determine how much fuel is used for personal transportation versus business purposes. If a truck driver uses their truck 80% for personal transportation and 20% for business transportation (based on mileage logged), then he or she can only take a deduction on 80% of the fuel costs (assuming they are operating as an LLC or sole proprietorship). If they are operating as a corporation or other type of business entity, then they can only take a deduction on the 20% of fuel costs that was used for business purposes.

Chapter 6: Regulation and Certification

This chapter will briefly discuss the different types of certification available to the owner-operator truck driver. It will also discuss the purpose of each type and how it is achieved. We will also touch on the regulation of the trucking industry which occurs under the Federal Motor Carrier Safety Administration (FMCSA).

It is important for the new truck business owner to understand the type of certification he or she will need to operate their business.

There are several types of certification that apply to the trucking industry. Each of these certifications have different requirements and purposes, but they all share a common goal: The safety and security of trucking operations. Truck drivers must be certified in order to operate the heavy equipment they are operating on our highways and roadways.

The Regulatory Landscape

The regulatory landscape for trucking businesses is a complex web of laws and regulations. This section will briefly describe the federal and state regulations that affect the trucking industry.

A number of federal regulations apply to the trucking industry:

Federal Motor Carrier Safety Regulations (FMCSRs)

These are the laws governing commercial motor vehicle operations within the United States. The FMCSRs are issued by the FMCSA and cover everything from driver qualification standards to vehicle maintenance standards. There is a set of rules within this category for interstate and intrastate drivers, cargo, vehicle operation, road transportation safety, and administrative procedures. All companies who operate in interstate commerce must comply with these rules.

Federal Highway Administration (FHWA) Regulations

The FHWA administers the Federal-aid Highway Program for the Federal Highway Administration, which is a division of the United States Department of Transportation.

Federal Railroad Administration (FRA) Regulations

The Federal Railroad Administration (FRA) regulates railroads and other rail carriers to ensure that they operate in a safe manner. The FRA also works to ensure that railroad employees work in a safe environment. It works to protect the general public by regulating issues such as train cars, locomotives, and railroad equipment. In addition, it regulates activities related to rail travel such as: inspections, safety procedures, rules of conduct for employees, employee qualifications for railroad jobs, and medical examination of employees.

State Regulations

State regulations vary from state to state; however, there are a number of similarities between states. For example, drivers need to maintain a CDL (commercial driver's license), which allows them to operate heavy trucks and other commercial vehicles in the state. Another common regulation is that all drivers must be trained and certified to operate the vehicle they are operating, whether it is an 18-wheeler or an automobile.

At this point you may be asking yourself "What about my state?" or "What about my county?" The answer is that most states have their own set of regulations for trucking businesses; however, there are some similarities across the board.

Certification Procedures

In order to operate a trucking business, you will need a driver who is properly certified to drive your vehicle(s). You will need him or her to be able to pass all driving tests as well as any required medical exams. In addition, you will need him or her to be qualified by your insurance company and legal authorities in order for him or her to legally transport your goods. There are several certification procedures that you will need to follow in order for your driver(s) to legally drive their truck(s). These procedures can vary greatly from one area of the country to another; however, there are some similarities.

The following is a brief description of some of the more common certification procedures for trucking businesses:

Driver Exam

All drivers must pass a knowledge exam and a driving test in order to obtain their CDL (commercial driver's license). To pass the test, drivers are required to pass an exam that covers regulations and safety issues such as hours of service,

151

inspection of vehicles, enforcement issues, and other regulations. The driver testing can be administered by the FMCSA, state licensing agency, or private organization such as Red Seal. There are different certification levels which include an air brake endorsement for drivers who wish to operate air brake equipped vehicles. Drivers who wish to drive only non-air equipment do not need any additional endorsements on their CDLs.

Medical Exam

All drivers must be medically certified before they are allowed to drive any commercial vehicle on public roads; however this is not always the case depending on the state you live in. For example, some states require all commercial vehicle operators (CMV) to have medical certifications while other states only require those over a certain age or those with specific medical conditions to have them. The FMCSA guidelines state that all CMV must have a valid medical certificate. To obtain this certificate, drivers need to visit a licensed healthcare professional and provide the license with all necessary information. After the information is reviewed by the healthcare professional, they may then issue a medical card and/or a certificate that allows them to drive for up to one year.

Vehicle Inspection

All commercial vehicles must be inspected before being allowed to operate on public roads. This inspection is usually carried out by a state agency that will examine the vehicle's brakes, lights, tires, etc. They will also check the driver's documents and make sure that all laws are being followed.

These inspections can vary by state; however, most states require an annual inspection for all commercial vehicles.

Business Licensing

As we discussed earlier in this chapter, there are several types of certification available to owner-operators who wish to become self-employed truck drivers. The type of certification you choose depends on how you want your business to operate; however, it is important for you to apply for any business licensing required by your state. If you are unsure whether or not you need business licensing in your area just contact your local government offices and ask them if there are any regulations in place regarding commercial transportation businesses operating within their jurisdictions. This way you can be sure that you aren't breaking any laws and you can avoid receiving a fine or having to pay a fee.

Commercial Driver's License and Medical Certification

The first certification that truck drivers must obtain is their Commercial Driver's License (CDL). This license is issued by the state in which the driver resides. The requirements vary from state to state. Some states require that a person be at least 18 years old, while others require you to be 21 years or older.

Some states also require that a person be a resident of the state for a certain period in order to qualify for a CDL. In addition to age and residency requirements, most states require that truck drivers have some type of certification for their Class A or B CDL's. This certification is obtained through an examination process administered by the state.

The exams are made up of several different sections including: air brakes, combination vehicles, non-CDL general knowledge, pre-trip inspection, and weight limits and restrictions. Each section has its own objectives and each one counts equally toward your final score on the exam.

Most states have adopted a "points" system in order to qualify for your CDL license. There are different point values assigned to each section of the exam as well as passing or failing status during your test session with your examiner (if you fail you will receive no points). The total points are calculated and if you have enough points, you will be issued your CDL license.

The second certification that truck drivers must have is their Medical Certification. State law requires that all truck drivers must have a current medical certification card on them at all times while they are driving. If they do not, the driver can be ticketed by the police or other law enforcement agencies.

The National Registry of Certified Medical Examiners (NRCME) is the only agency that issues these cards to drivers. These cards are valid for five years and must be renewed every five years in order for the driver to remain certified.

A driver's medical exam is usually more thorough than an ordinary physical. The purpose of this exam is to protect the public from unsafe drivers who may cause accidents because of their health conditions or impairment from drugs or alcohol. The medical examiner will take your blood pressure, check your eyesight, listen to your heart and lungs, check your ears and nose, etc. In addition, he or she will also take your blood for drug and alcohol testing as well as a urinalysis test for drug testing (this is done on site).

In order to acquire your medical certification card you must pass this examination with a minimum of a "moderately acceptable" score. If you score in the lowest level, you will be rejected and will have to retake the exam again until you have scored at a higher level of "moderately acceptable."

The National Registry does not publish an average score for their examinations. This is done to avoid giving drivers an idea of the minimum score they must achieve to pass. It is possible that if all drivers knew the average score many would try to take the test when they were not yet ready to do so. The medical examiner will also inform your employer when you receive your medical certification card so that they can authorize your employment and write it on your job application.

Remember, if you become sick in between physicals or lose your card, you must contact NRCME immediately. If they do not hear from you, they will assume that you have quit driving and notified your employer that he or she can no longer find work for you since the status has changed on their computer files (since driver records are computerized). This could also lead to a future unemployment claim against your policy if it is found out that you are not actively employed as a driver (in some cases) when an accident occurs.

Federal Motor Carrier Safety Administration

The Federal Motor Carrier Safety Administration (FMCSA) is a government agency that regulates the trucking industry. Its role is to ensure the safety of all drivers and vehicles on our roadways. This agency makes up the majority of our safety and security regulations in this industry.

The FMCSA issues certificates to qualified individuals through several programs. These certificates include:

- Driver's License
- Commercial Driver's License (CDL)
- Certificate of Inspection (COI)
- Medical Examiner Certificate (MEC)

Each of these certifications have different requirements, but they all contribute to the overall safety and security of the trucking industry.

Driver's License

This is the most common type of certification in the trucking industry. The licenses are issued by the Department of Motor Vehicles (DMV) in each state.

Every driver must have a license to operate large trucks on U.S. roads and highways. However, some states allow non-resident drivers to get licensed if they drive the same amount of time as resident drivers during their period in that state. For example, if a driver wants to get licensed in Florida, he or she must drive within Florida for at least 30 days before taking a state driving exam.

The state driving exam is a requirement for all drivers. It must be taken in every state they want to get licensed in. The exam is a measure of the applicant's knowledge of the state traffic laws and regulations.

There are also requirements for those who want to get licensed in a truck or bus category (Class A, B, or C). They must have passed a CDL knowledge test that covers their chosen category and rules for interstate commerce. The test is 100 questions long, and it has to be taken in front of an official examiner from the DMV.

CDL

This type of certification is required by all drivers who operate heavy trucks on our roads and highways. These trucks include 18-wheelers, forklifts, dump trucks, etc. A CDL is issued by the FMCSA through their licensing program. It allows drivers to operate their vehicles across state lines under federal rules and regulations. It also allows them to drive large trucks for hire (as opposed to personal use). This means that they can drive commercial vehicles such as passenger buses or school buses on any given day if they have a CDL permit. Trucking companies can hire these drivers for temporary or permanent positions.

The CDL exam is similar to the state driving exam, but it has more questions on a wider range of topics. It is not just a test of state traffic laws and regulations, but it also covers federal rules and regulations and safety requirements specific to commercial vehicles. It has to be taken in front of an official examiner from the DMV.

As mentioned earlier, the CDL requires two exams: Knowledge and Skills. The knowledge exam is 100 questions long, and it must be taken in front of an official FMCSA examiner. The skills exam can be taken on public roads or at a state-approved truck driving school. The skills exam is 100 questions long, and it covers every aspect of truck operation required by the FMCSA for Class A drivers (18-wheelers). For example: steering the vehicle, backing up safely, shifting gears properly, etc.

Certificate of Inspection (COI)

This certificate is required by all drivers who operate heavy trucks on our roads and highways under Federal Motor Carrier Safety Regulations (FMCSR). This certificate verifies that each vehicle meets federal safety standards for commercial motor vehicles (CMVs) before it can be used on public highways. These safety standards include:

- Brakes (including ABS braking systems)
- Steering mechanisms (power steering, etc.)
- Seat belts
- Mirrors and glass (windshield, side windows, and rear window)
- Clutch operation (and foot pedal adjustment if applicable)
- Air brake system components and air lines.

The COI is issued by the FMCSA through their licensing program. It allows drivers to operate their vehicles across state lines under federal rules and regulations.

To issue a COI, the vehicle must pass an inspection by an FMCSA-approved inspector. This official will then issue a COI providing proof that the vehicle meets all federal safety standards. The COI is valid for one year from its date of issuance.

The vehicle must be inspected every time it is sold or transferred. The new owner can use the same inspection report as long as he or she does not make any changes to the vehicle before getting it inspected again. If changes are made, a new inspection report must be issued by an FMCSA-approved inspector before the vehicle can be used for commercial purposes on highways and roads in the United States.

Port State Measures Agreements (PSMA)

The PSMA is an international agreement between countries in which the countries agree to work together to improve safety and security of the trucking industry. It was signed by 53 countries, including the United States.

The PSMA is administered by the International Maritime Organization (IMO). The IMO creates and enforces new regulations that apply to all participating countries. These regulations are designed to enhance safety, security, environmental protection, and social responsibility in the global maritime industry.

The PSMA requires countries to have a National Authority for implementation. The National Authority is a government agency that works with the trucking industry in order to ensure that the country's laws and regulations meet the requirements of the PSMA.

The United States has created its own National Authority, called the Federal Motor Carrier Safety Administration (FMCSA). The FMCSA is responsible for regulating all commercial motor vehicles in the US. It enforces PSMA regulations.

PSMA regulations cover all heavy commercial vehicles and vehicles being used to transport hazardous materials. These vehicles must be properly maintained and operated according to international standards. There are several types of certification that apply to truck drivers:

Driver Qualification Certificate

This certificate is required by international agreement, and it certifies that drivers have been trained properly in order to operate a truck on a regular basis on public roads. The Driver Qualification Certificate is also known as an International Driver's Permit or IDP. It functions like a passport for commercial vehicle drivers who need to cross borders into different countries on a regular basis. It also provides an additional layer of security for trucking companies and carriers who hire drivers from other countries. By using this IDP, the company can ensure that the driver they hired is well-trained and will not put themselves, other drivers, or the public in danger.

International Certificate of Vaccination

This certificate is issued by governments to ensure that truck drivers have been properly vaccinated against infectious disease before they are allowed to operate their vehicles on the roadways. It certifies that the driver has been properly immunized against specific diseases, such as tetanus and hepatitis. This certificate is required by international agreements and regulations, including the PSMA. It is often required by individual countries when a driver needs entry into a foreign country.

International Medical Certificate

This certificate certifies that drivers have been examined by a medical professional who has certified that they are healthy enough to operate heavy commercial vehicles on public roads. The International Medical Certificate is only valid for one year. During this time period, it must be renewed every year with proof of continued medical examination and certification. The IMC is also known as an International Road User Card or IRU card.

International Driver's License

This license is a translation of a driver's home country license. It is used by drivers who need to operate a commercial vehicle in another country. It is also known as an International Driving Permit or IDP.

Transportation Worker Identification Credential Card

This certificate certifies that drivers have been properly trained and certified in order to operate maritime facilities. These vehicles include tankers, buses, and other heavy commercial vehicles inside dock warehouses and port offices. The TWIC Card is valid for five years. During this time period, it must be renewed every five years with proof of continued certification.

How to File a FMCSA Complaint

If you have a complaint about a trucking company that you believe violates the law, the Federal Motor Carrier Safety Administration (FMCSA) is the agency to contact. This is the federal government agency which regulates all aspects of interstate and intrastate trucking.

Here are the steps you should follow to file a FMCSA complaint:

The first step is to obtain the FMCSA complaint form. You may request this form by calling 1-800-832-5660 and requesting it or you may print out a copy from the FMCSA website at: http://www.fmcsa.dot.gov

The second step is to fill out the form completely and accurately. The information you provide in your complaint will be used to investigate your complaint. Be sure to include your name and address so that the investigators can contact you if needed. You should also include the name and address of the trucking company that is involved in your complaint, as well as a detailed description of what happened along with any supporting documents such as photographs, invoices, etc.

The third step is to send your completed complaint form and supporting documentation to:

Federal Motor Carrier Safety Administration (FMCSA) Office of Enforcement Analysis and Evaluation (OEAE) Document Control Center Attn: Administrative Support Section 11501 Blue Ridge Blvd., Suite 1200 Fairfax, VA 22033

The fourth step is to await the results of the investigation. This process may take several months and, in some cases, it takes longer than that. The FMCSA will contact you when the investigation is complete. If you do not receive a response from the FMCSA within 60 days, you can contact them by phone or by email.

If you receive a response to your complaint from the FMCSA, it will include information about what they have done to address your complaint and a date for when they completed their investigation. If you are not satisfied with their response, you can request a review of their decision by contacting them again.

When contacting the FMCSA, remember that no one there is required to assist you or give you any information unless your complaint has been filed using the official form and has been deemed valid by the agency. The agency is under no legal obligation to provide you with any assistance except when filing a valid FMCSA complaint form.

Conclusion

We have come to the end of the book and hope that you have enjoyed reading it as much as we enjoyed writing it. We feel that we have answered most of your questions about what is involved in running an owner-operator trucking business in this book.

We would like to thank you for taking the time to read our book and hope that you found it informative and helpful in your ambitions to run your own trucking business.

Setting up and operating a trucking business is one of the most rewarding and satisfying things you can do. You are your own boss, you set your own schedule, you set your own pay.

As the saying goes "there is more than one way to skin a cat" and there is more than one way to run an owner-operator trucking business, but we have tried to lay out the facts and the steps that got us where we are today. If you have any alternative methods or ideas feel free to pass them on.

Good luck with your trucking business!

* 9 7 8 1 9 5 5 4 2 3 2 2 9 *